PUBLICITY FOR FREE

HOW TO GET

PUBLICITY FOR FREE

How to write a press release, contact the media, gain radio and television interviews, and organise press conferences

DAVID NORTHMORE

BLOOMSBURY

First published 1993 by Bloomsbury Publishing Limited, 2 Soho Square, London W1V 5DE

Copyright © 1993 by David Northmore

The moral right of the author has been asserted

A CIP record for this book is available from the British Library

ISBN 0 7475 0833 X

Typeset by Hewer Text Composition Services, Edinburgh
Printed in England by Clays Ltd, St Ives plc

Contents

About the author

David Northmore is an experienced civil rights campaigner and publicist who has been at the forefront of a number of major civil liberties campaigns in recent years. These have included campaigns concerning freedom of information, censorship and lesbian and gay rights.

A regular contributor to the *Guardian*, David Northmore has also written for the *Independent*, *Observer*, *Sunday Correspondent*, *New Statesman and Society*, *Gay Times*, *Local Government Chronicle* and the *UK Press Gazette*. In the early 1980s he also wrote a regular column for the *Kent Evening Post*.

He has broadcast on freedom of information issues on BBC Television, Channel 4, TVS, BBC Radios 2, 4 and 5, LBC, BBC World Service, British Forces Broadcasting Service and numerous local and regional radio stations. His first book, *The Freedom of Information Handbook*, was published by Bloomsbury in April 1990 and received the *Reference Reviews* Best General Reference Book 1990 award.

Introduction

'For knowledge itself is power', proclaimed the writer Francis Bacon (1561–1626). Hundreds of years later another writer, Edward Bulwer Lytton (1803–1873), is credited as saying: 'The pen is mightier than the sword'. They were both right, and since those declarations were first written many politicians, authors and journalists have taken them as their own.

There can be no doubt that we live in a media-dominated society: elections are won and lost on television; politicians can be ruined overnight in the press; entertainers become instant successes because of carefully manipulated public relations campaigns – usually in the popular national tabloid newspapers. It all depends upon who is pulling the media strings and, surprisingly, any of us is able to obtain media coverage for our particular cause or event. The publicity techniques for a celebrity engaging on a new escapade are largely the same for a community group protesting about a local problem.

Anyone can get publicity for free: artists, religious groups, businesspeople, trade unionists, gay rights activists, politicians, multinational companies, councillors, authors, environmentalists, voluntary groups, models, lawyers, government departments, spies – and ordinary men, women and children who have never been involved with the media before. In fact, anyone with a point of view on almost any subject will be able to express that view to the world somehow through newspapers, magazines, radio stations and television networks.

This handbook is aimed at anyone who wishes to obtain publicity at any level: from a community group wishing to make a small announcement in the local newspaper, through to bigger campaigning or commercial organizations aiming to build up a major publicity campaign on a nationwide scale. Whether you are an amateur or professional, you can learn how to get publicity for free.

Why, though, get publicity for free? The answer to that question is painfully simple: the alternative to free publicity is expensive publicity – or advertising, as it is better known. Some institutions can afford to pay tens of thousands of pounds to take out full-page adverts in the national press: British Nuclear Fuels, for example, or some of the bigger public sector trade unions such as the National and Local Government Officers' Association (NALGO). But they are rare examples. Many organizations and most individuals are unable to afford the luxury of paid advertising, but they still have a legitimate message to pass on to the rest of society and the right to make their views known. However, they can all use a simple publicity technique – known as the press release – to inform the newspapers, radio stations and television broadcasters of their message, and provide the journalists and broadcasters with the necessary information from which articles and programmes can be produced.

A press release, which is the centre of all publicity – whether intended as a short notice in the local newspaper or an in-depth investigative feature article in a national newspaper – is a short written statement sent to news editors. It contains a brief outline of the issues, written in a set journalistic style, and provides journalists with other essential information, such as direct quotes, facts and figures, and the phone number of the person who can be contacted for more details if necessary.

But one word of caution: there is no absolute guarantee that your story will make it into the local newspaper or on to the neighbourhood radio station. There is a huge publicity industry, known as public relations or PR, which earns millions of pounds each year – mainly from big business – by obtaining publicity for the goods or services those businesses offer. However, the vast bulk of PR material sent to newspapers and other media organizations ends up in the wastepaper bin, as the trained journalistic eye can identify PR material at one hundred paces; it is usually very glossy, very bulky and printed to a very high standard on the best quality paper. A 'straight' press release – although neat and well presented – will normally be no more than two photocopied sheets of A4 stapled in the top left-hand corner. Journalists have a nose for 'hard news' but are very cautious about glossy PR handouts. Chapter 1 of this guide explains in detail how to write a press release, and anyone who can read and write will be able to produce a press release that stands a greater chance of being read by a journalist than the glossy PR handouts.

For most users of this handbook the principal media targets will be the local newspapers, radio and television stations – and the regional newspapers. If national newspapers do report stories with a strong local source then it is usually because they are picked up by a news agency or the national newspaper itself. There is normally little benefit for anyone with a local story to send it to a national newspaper, as it will probably join the many hundreds of PR press releases and handouts received by each national newspaper every day. There are, of course, exceptions to every rule.

Here are some examples of individuals and groups that have generated substantial publicity by using one or two very simple publicity-generating techniques:

- Want to buy a submarine? Those were the words on the lips of Ron Hadley of the Inter Action Social Enterprise Trust which owned the 300-foot HMS *Sea Lion* submarine. The trust bought the vessel from the Ministry of Defence with the intention of converting it into a museum and educational base. But the trust was unable to obtain the necessary financial backing, and so it had no choice but to put HMS *Sea Lion* on the market. But how do you sell a submarine? Simple. Place a huge 'For Sale' sign on the bow and issue a brief one-page press release. The resulting free publicity in the press and on radio and television news programmes secured a buyer for the £200,000 submarine in record time – and there was no estate agent's fee to pay!

● Publicity was something that Colin Smith desperately needed to obtain in order to achieve a substantial pay rise. A fifteen-year-old newspaper delivery boy, Colin realized that he was being paid only a quarter of the rate that an adult received for doing the same work. So Colin joined a trade union, became a shop steward and started to campaign for better rates of pay. A local newspaper reported Colin's campaign, a local news agency then picked up the story and Colin soon attracted nationwide publicity in the press and on the radio and television.

● That type of nationwide publicity was exactly what environmental campaigners were looking for when they launched a protest at a planning inquiry into proposals to build a nuclear power station near their town. So one of them dressed up as a clown as she clearly thought the inquiry was a judicial circus – and silently sprinkled mock radioactive dust around the inquiry. This cheap and easily staged publicity stunt attracted considerable media publicity – particularly in the tabloid newspapers. So too did Darth Varder, from the film *Star Wars*, when he made an appearance outside the Department of the Environment's London offices. The government had granted planning permission to a Hollywood entertainments conglomerate to build a movie theme park on London's largest designated Site of Special Scientific Interest. A supporter of Friends of the Earth, this particular Darth Varder held up a placard that read simply 'We demand a public inquiry'. If nothing else, he certainly gained widespread publicity that was most embarrassing for the government.

- High-profile events intended to attract extensive media publicity need not be costly or time-consuming to stage. Following a controversial and unpopular Supreme Court decision in the United States that restricted the rights of women to have abortions, a small number of protesters outside the Supreme Court building held up wire coathangers with notes attached that read 'The do-it-yourself abortion kit'. The protest gained international coverage, including considerable attention in the British press. Imaginative Paraguayan protesters also gained wide coverage at a reception for Pope John Paul II at the beginning of a state visit to Paraguay in 1988. Complaining about state repression and censorship, some members of the 3000-strong audience that greeted the Pope wore bandanas across their mouths to symbolize their inability to speak freely.

With a little imagination and work almost any type of cause or organization can gain publicity for free. This handbook shows how any individual or organization – from a small neighbourhood group through to large international concerns – can do so.

1

What is news?

Almost any event – or anybody – can be news. An event does not have to be of world-shattering importance to get into print or reach the airwaves. Indeed, the more popular newspapers and broadcasters are often criticized for covering 'non-stories', or stories that are extremely trivial. Seemingly everyday events, though, make the news on a routine basis. To demonstrate that point one national newspaper diary column attempted to amuse its readers by running a 'boring headline' competition. Entries included:

'Bexhill resident aged 89 dies suddenly'
Bexhill News

'Cyclist had to brake'
Kentish Gazette

'Church clock did not stop 40 years ago'
The Messenger, Stockport

'Oswestry mayor plants a tree'
Shropshire Star

'Former deputy mayor of Rugby twin-town dies'
Rugby Advertiser

'Liechtenstein's exports fall by 0.6%'
Financial Times

'World has warmed by 0.4 degrees since 1965'
The Times

'Fish and chips enjoyed at Edgbaston Women Zionists
Bazaar'
Birmingham Jewish Recorder

The winner, however, could have been a news story reported
in the *Guardian* Diary from the *Eastern Evening News* with the
headline 'Police called to halt goat havoc', which started:
'Rampaging goats have caused chaos in Bowthorpe, where
church services have been disrupted by goats peering through
windows at the congregation.'

What is news?

It has been said that news is something that somebody
somewhere does not want to see in print – although the above
examples of headlines indicate that newspapers are sometimes
not spoiled for choice; there is often not enough solid, hard
news to fill every column of every page of the newspaper.
However, a news story should ideally contain three essential
ingredients. They are:

●   Human interest

●   Topicality

●   Conflict

Let us look at each of those ingredients in detail.

Human interest
This, as the heading suggests, means that the theme of the
press release – and the resulting news items – must relate to
people. Either the centre of the story must *be* a person, or the
topic of the story must *affect* people in some way. For
example, if the story is about a local person complaining
about an environmental hazard, then we have an instant

'human interest' story; the human interest being the complaining person – assuming that the individual concerned is either the victim of the hazard, or in some way represents the victims or the affected community. Similarly, if the central theme of the story is a government proposal to build a six-lane elevated motorway through your neighbourhood, then the 'human interest' angle of the story is the potential victims – the local residents.

All publicity should ideally contain a human interest element, and most publicity planned by individuals or local groups will automatically have such an angle. It is only when dealing with particularly technical subjects that the human angle fails to appear: a government department that plans to build a nuclear electricity generating plant, for example, will find it very difficult to create a human interest angle for its publicity. Its opponents, however, will have no such difficulty. The stories of potential victims obviously have a strong human interest angle; many pressure groups are very experienced at presenting ordinary people as the unwitting victims of all manner of wrongdoings and injustices. But don't be fooled that the 'human' in human interest has to be human at all! ITN's *News at Ten* programme demonstrated this for many years, filling the humorous slot at the end of each programme with a variety of animals engaged in strange pursuits, such as skateboarding ducks or parrots that drink beer. Animals can be humans in the eyes of the media.

Topicality

Topicality is simple to explain: for an issue to have any news worthiness it must have some relevance to the present – to today, or perhaps to earlier or later this week. It is, essentially, about *now*! For the lay person issuing a press release it is the easiest news quality to manipulate, because the mere fact that someone is issuing a press statement in the form of a press release actually creates the topicality. This is rather like when the television newscaster says 'Buckingham Palace today announced that . . .' Often the newsmaker has the advantage of dictating the agenda – *you* decide why your press release is being issued today, and not this time next week or last month.

Conflict

Conflict is perhaps the most important of all news ingredients: anything from a full-scale nuclear war to a dispute between neighbours contains some element of conflict. Or, to put it another way, there is little in the way of reported news that is the *opposite* of conflict, such as 'happy' news or 'good' news. Either such news is regarded as trivial, or it attracts criticism and instantly becomes standard conflict-ridden news. A story about a well-known zoo animal having a baby will certainly make a good photo-opportunity in the national press; however, a story about a zoo animal that escapes from the zoo and terrorizes the surrounding area will probably make the front pages until it is caught. Therefore, the conflict element adds considerably to the news value.

If your proposed press release contains all three of these ingredients – human interest, topicality and conflict – then there is a strong possibility that your item will appear in print or be heard on the airwaves. However, a story will stand if it has any two of those three ingredients. Even the *Guardian*'s 'Police called to halt goat havoc' story managed to include all three: 'Rampaging goats have caused chaos in Bowthorpe, where church services have been disrupted by goats peering through windows at the congregation.' The human interest is the congregation (although it *could* be the goats); the topicality is that at the time of publication it was a recent event; and the conflict is the self-assumed difficulty experienced by the congregation at being observed at prayer by otherwise harmless goats.

Why get publicity?

It has been said that there are people in this world who obtain publicity simply because they like to see their names in print or their faces on the television screen. This may be so. But there are a number of other quite legitimate reasons for obtaining publicity. They include:

Attracting attention

This will be the main reason that most people will want to obtain publicity in the press and broadcast media – simply to draw attention to a cause or event. This could be to alert a community about that six-lane elevated motorway, or a variety of important issues that should be reported in the press and about which the public has a right to know. Although attracting attention may seem one of the most obvious reasons for obtaining publicity, it also provides a valuable public service: the public should have the right to know what is going on in the world around them; groups and individuals within society should have the freedom to express their opinions on most – if not all – subjects; and the newspapers and broadcasting organizations should be available to the public to allow a range of opinions to be expressed and for debates to take place.

Promoting your service or company

It is not only issues of public concern that can be promoted by attracting publicity, but more commercial matters too. A company of any size, ranging from a multi-national employing many thousands of people, through to a sole trader, is able to use the press release and other publicity techniques to promote the goods or services that it provides. However, generating news – as distinct from responding to news – is a more difficult task, but one that can be overcome. As we saw earlier, the victims of an event – be it an incident at a nuclear power station or an environmental hazard – are instant news stories in themselves. But consider, for example, that you plan to open a flower shop in the High Street. How do you go about getting publicity in the press for free?

A straightforward press release announcing the opening of your shop will generate little publicity – maybe one short paragraph in the 'News in Brief' column of the local newspaper. It may also generate a call from the newspaper's advertising sales department inviting you to buy advertising space. But there are ways that the florist could generate coverage in the editorial pages of the local newspaper and on the local radio and television stations. Here are two examples:

- Call on the Mayor! Why not invite the local Mayor to open the shop? By sending out such an invitation, one of two events will come about: either she agrees to open the shop and automatically generates the publicity that accompanies such dignitaries; or she refuses, in which case you have all the necessary ingredients for a standard news story (remember the human interest–topicality–conflict formula). A little imagination could produce a press release headed: 'Florist slams Mayor for High Street business apathy' – or something similar.

- Make a floral sculpture. Why not make an original and distinctive floral sculpture of a local landmark – such as a castle, or lighthouse, or a symbolic design of local significance? Once done, the sculpture can be donated to the children's ward of a local hospital, or a hospice, or home for the elderly. Hey presto! – we have a perfect photo-opportunity that the news editor will find hard to resist. It would be even more difficult to resist if the town's Mayor can be pursuaded to present the floral sculpture!

These are just two examples of how one tradesperson might be able to attract publicity in the local press and broadcast media – maybe filling an amount of editoral space equivalent to several hundreds of pounds' worth of advertising space. A little brainstorming and imagination will enable almost any type of trader or professional to generate publicity for free.

Recruiting members or supporters

Political parties, pressure groups, charities, sports teams, campaigning organizations and voluntary groups all rely on their members for their existence. Indeed, such organizations *are* their members, and they will all need to attract new blood from time to time. Occasionally they may also need specialist help. For example, a church may need the services of a voluntary driver to help with a senior citizens' club; a charity may need the services of an accountant; or perhaps a local Sunday League football team needs extra team members. Such groups can obtain free publicity to inform the local community of its activities and its practical needs.

Fundraising

Where would the Great Ormond Street Hospital for Sick Children 'Wishing Well' appeal be if it were not for press and media coverage? Well, it probably would not exist at all if there was no free publicity, as the public would not know about it – and, hence, no fundraising. Many charities, hospitals, social services and other appeals rely upon public donations, and those appeals in turn rely upon the publicity generated by the media for the public to help them reach their targets. Newspaper editors and broadcasters are often keen to be seen promoting worthy causes as it helps their own image and, naturally, may also help to sell newspapers and boost audience figures.

The golden rules of publicity

Before starting to put together a publicity campaign, or even a one-off press release, there are four key rules that the would-be publicist should consider. Each of these should be studied in detail as they may save the non-professional publicist considerable anxiety and inconvenience – and may even prevent unwelcome legal action.

Golden rule 1: Don't do it!

Some people thrive on generating publicity and basking in the attention that it brings; others hate it. However glamorous being under the publicity spotlight may appear at first sight –

even if it is only in your local newspaper – do give some
thought to the consequences of such new-found fame:
journalists may telephone you at all hours to consult or
interview you on the latest developments of your story; press
stories may be chased up by radio and television journalists –
even if you did not send them a press release; and always bear
in mind that local stories can be picked up by national
newspapers very quickly. Many news stories that appear on
the radio or television are discovered by broadcast journalists
who read the local newspapers. (You can always refuse to do
a radio or television interview if you wish, but that will not
stop the calls from coming); your photograph may appear in
the press; your story may attract denials, rebuttals or counter-
claims – thereby generating more work for you in the form of
further interviews or letters to the Letters to the Editor
column. In short, only ever send out a press release if you are
prepared to see it through to the end.

Golden rule 2: Do the journalists' job for them

Journalists are always under considerable pressure of work,
and that pressure has increased noticeably in recent years.
There are two main reasons for this. Firstly, there has been a
huge increase in the number of media organizations in this
country: the development of satellite and cable television; the
growth in the number of local and regional radio stations; an
increase in the number of newspaper titles published around
the country; plans for an additional national television
channel; plans for nationwide independent radio stations; and
a growth in the number of freelance journalists and press
agencies serving the community. But, at the same time, there
has been a drastic reduction in the number of journalists
working in this growth industry – mainly because the
economic conditions of the late 1980s and early 1990s resulted
in a sizeable reduction in the amount of advertising revenue
being earned by newspapers and commercial broadcast organizations. This, though, provides the ideal opportunity for the
publicist to increase the likelihood of his or her press release
being used; simply, if you do the bulk of the journalist's job

for her, including getting together as much of the background research as possible, then all she has to do is write up the story. This substantially increases the chances of your story appearing in print, and is perhaps one of the most useful points of all to remember when planning a publicity campaign of any size. Remember, journalists need you as much as you need them.

Golden rule 3: Get the facts right

This might sound like obvious advice, but even prominent public figures have been known to make themselves look complete idiots simply by getting their facts wrong. Normally it only results in a little short-lived public embarrassment. But occasionally it can result in the threat of a libel writ, which is well worth avoiding. To avoid such problems do check your facts and figures thoroughly – including any information given to you by your opponent or even official bodies – at least twice before relying on them. Also, ensure that other details, such as personal names and dates, are accurate. If it helps, then keep key facts and figures handy in a notebook or on a card so they can be easily consulted when being interviewed.

Golden rule 4: Keep it legal

There are generally three areas of the law that concern writers and journalists, and which equally apply to anyone putting out publicity material. They are: libel; obscenity; and official secrecy.

●   **Libel**: this is the most common of the legal pitfalls to face the writer, although the publicist is safeguarded by one crucial element: media organizations know the hazards of libel and, as much for their own sakes as for any others', will normally filter everything for libel before going to press. However, it is also libellous to communicate a defamatory statement in a press release that is not even used by a newspaper or broadcasting organization. Although libel only applies to individuals, as distinct from companies or official bodies, if in doubt, leave it out.

- **Obscenity**: the communication of any material that may be considered indecent or obscene can be subject to a variety of obscure and often contradictory laws. This could, for example, be a problem for a regional arts centre or gallery staging exhibitions of visual or performing arts. Beauty, after all, is in the eye of the beholder; but as this is a weak legal defence always consult appropriate civil rights organizations or lawyers for advice.

- **Official secrets**: although the need for official secrecy is reducing by the month, the State is still prepared to flex its judicial muscles to gag writers and publishers – as the now infamous *Spycatcher* case demonstrated. Unless you work with alleged official secrets and are planning to become a whistleblower, then it is unlikely that your publicity campaign will breach the Official Secrets Act. If you do, and you are, then do take legal advice from a solicitor before proceeding.

Few publicity campaigns will result in any form of legal action, as most are based on 'fair comment' – a legal term meaning that the statement in question is true, or based on reasonable opinion and without malice – such as the public interest and individual comment. But one slip of the pen can easily cause seemingly endless legal problems. Check and check again; if necessary take legal advice.

Finally, although publicity can be free, and although there are often many opportunities to obtain publicity in newspapers and on radio and television programmes, there is of course no guarantee that the media will use your story. There may be a number of reasons for this: it could be that you chose a busy news day and there was not enough time or space to use your story. Or perhaps your press release was not produced in a sufficiently eye-catching style or arrived too late to be used.

All publicists – both professional and amateur – experience rejection at one time or another. It is more of an art than a science to generate publicity successfully, and the media industry is a huge and often impersonal world. So don't take any rejection or failure personally. If it happens to you then you will need to sit back and spend some time analysing what, if anything, went wrong. A little time spent in this way will increase the chances of your next publicity campaign being a success. A civil rights activist once put out a press release announcing a major legal victory in parliament over the right to demonstrate in public – proposals in a parliamentary bill that aimed to impose bureaucratic conditions on existing rights to demonstrate were thrown out by a committee of MPs. The press release was well written; the story was highly topical and the whole subject was very controversial – it had attracted media coverage when the proposals had originally surfaced. But not one newspaper or broadcasting organization publicized the victory. The reason was that the wrong date had been typed at the top of press release, and journalists simply thought that it was an old document that had somehow resurfaced a year later. Humans can often make the news, but they can also make mistakes. Check every detail carefully!

How to get publicity for free – publicity checklist

- You can make the news. News is all about people like *you*. You too can get your news story into print and on the airwaves with a little work and imagination.
- Promote your cause. Whether you are running a business, charity or campaign – or simply have something to get off your chest – you can contact newspapers, radio and television stations by issuing a press release, the key to publicity.
- They want to hear from you. Today there are a record number of newspapers, radio stations and television channels all hungry for news and programme ideas.

- Help the journalists help you. By researching and preparing your material carefully you can hugely increase the chances of your press release being used.
- Be careful! Get your facts right and double-check them. Ensure that you avoid any legal pitfalls by following a few simple guidelines and taking legal advice if in doubt.

2

The press release

A press release is a written statement from the person or organization aiming to achieve publicity in newspapers and on radio and television stations. It is written in a set style that can be used directly by journalists to write a news story, and is the most important single tool available to the publicist. Therefore time and effort needs to be put into making the press release attractive and readily usable by reporters and sub-editors.

The advantages of using a press release

- You decide what you say to the press – and also what you don't say to the press – without any pressure from reporters.

- It is in writing, and therefore the content of a press release cannot be disputed later on.

- You control the timing of the publication of the press release, which can be to your advantage.

- It is helpful to the journalists to have a single document to work from.

- A press release is a cost-effective way of obtaining publicity; each one sent out will cost approximately 50p to produce.

● In short, it is *your* news and *you* can largely control it by using a press release.

Here is an example of a real press release issued by a trade union branch to the local media:

NATIONAL UNION OF PUBLIC EMPLOYEES

LOCAL ADDRESS
All Saints Hospital,
Chatham,
Kent,
ME4 5NG.
Tel: Medway (0634) 407311.   Ref:DAN/VJG/59.08

PRESS RELEASE : IMMEDIATE.   10th AUGUST, 1981.

PRIVATE AMBULANCES OPPOSED BY HOSPITAL STAFF

Members of the National Union of Public Employees in
Medways Hospitals are threatening to boycott private
ambulances in a campaign of active resistance to private
contractors in the National Health Service.

Medilink, of Boundry Road, Chatham, has recently started
a private ambulance service in the Medway Towns, in
addition to their courier and drug-running service which
is currently contracted to the Medway Health District.

District Secretary of NUPE, David Northmore, said:-

"It is disgusting to think that unqualified people
are able to tackle such responsible duties of life
or death without any monitor of their standard, and
without properly trained medical personnel available
in emergancies."

The Executive Committee of the Medway Hospitals Branch of
NUPE has resolved to fight against private sector takeover
of Health Service work in a bid to make savings in the
already underfunded Medway Health District.

Mr.Northmore continued:-

"We are strongly advising our 750 members in the District
to refuse to co-operate with 'Medilink' and we are making
representations to the District Management Team of
Medways Hospitals insisting that they don't renew the
contract with 'Medilink' in October, 1981."

- m.f. -

<u>Private Ambulances 2</u>

"The work being undertaken by Medilink must be taken
over by the Kent Ambulance Service. We are writing
to local MP's and the Health Service Minister, Gerald
Vaughn, stressing the urgent need for a massive
injection of funds into Medways antiquated and inadequate
hospitals."

Delegates from NUPE are meeting with representatives of the
nine other Unions in the Medway Health District to decide
what possible joint action can be organised to stop private
sector enterprise in the social responsibility of Health
Care.

ENDS

FOR FURTHER INFORMATION:

David Northmore.

Medway 407311 (office),
Medway 78293 (home).

And here is the front page of the local weekly newspaper some four days later:

The campaign launched by this particular press release continued for many weeks, generating coverage in all local newspapers and the two radio stations in the area.

What should go into a press release?

All journalists learn that every news story should contain the five 'W's. They are:

- **Who**

- **What**

- **Where**

- **When**

- **Why**

The opening paragraph of a press release – preferably the first sentence of it – should contain a succinct and straightforward outline of the story by using the first four of those 'W's. They are:

- **Who** (is doing it)

- **What** (is happening)

- **Where** (it is taking place)

- **When** (it is happening or has happened or will happen)

Let us look again at the opening paragraph of NUPE's successful press release:

> 'Members of the National Union of Public Employees in Medway's Hospitals are threatening to boycott private ambulances in a campaign of active resistance to private contractors in the National Health Service.'

This opening paragraph clearly contains the four key 'W's:

- **Who** (NUPE members)

- **What** (boycott of private ambulances)

- **Where** (Medway's hospitals)

- **When** (now, implied in 'threatening')

Here is another example of a press release, this time issued by a Member of Parliament to announce the introduction of a parliamentary Bill:

HOUSE OF COMMONS
LONDON SW1A 0AA

PRESS RELEASE: STRICTLY EMBARGOED - 00·01 WEDNESDAY DECEMBER 5 1990

REFORM OF SAFETY LAW WHICH 'WILL SAVE THOUSANDS OF LIVES' IS BACKED BY MAJORITY OF MP'S

A back bench MP who rated highly in the recent ballot for private members' Bills today introduces the Public Safety Information Bill to Parliament, which will reduce the chances of major disasters - such as Clapham Junction, King's Cross, Zeebrugge, Bradford and the sinking of the Marchioness - from recurring.

John Bowis, the Conservative MP for Battersea who came fourth in the ballot, is confident that the Public Safety Information Bill will become law as it has already attracted the unprecedented support of 368 MP's of all political parties in the House of Commons.

Announcing his decision, Mr Bowis today said: "No law can prevent the unforeseen disaster, but the law can ensure that the foreseeable is known to the public."

He continued: "I feel particularly strongly on this as the MP representing the Clapham Junction rail network where we had a terrible disaster two years ago, and with constituents affected by the King's Cross fire."

The Bill will require that information about any known threats to the public of physical injury is publicly displayed at the location of the hazard.

m. f.

Again, the four 'W's rule has been used:

- **Who** (a Member of Parliament)
- **What** (introduces Public Safety Information Bill)
- **Where** (Parliament)
- **When** (today)

The first paragraph of a press release is the most important part of the whole document as it has to grab the journalist's attention and imagination immediately and 'sell' the story idea to that particular media organization. The second paragraph can also be used to elaborate on the propositions contained in the first, if necessary.

'Why' is the fifth 'W', and asks 'why is this thing happening?' In the case of our examples the reason that NUPE members in Medway threatened to boycott private contractors in the NHS was not because they had nothing better to do. The reason, as the press release goes on to explain, is that they felt threatened by one particular private contractor operating in their hospitals at that time. Similarly, the reason that the MP introduced the Public Safety Information Bill was because of a major disaster that occurred in his constituency during the previous year.

The next two or three paragraphs can be used to explain *why* the details contained in the opening paragraph are going to take place. This should involve the use of direct quotes which are appreciated by journalists as they can be lifted directly into the resulting story.

Our Member of Parliament does this in the third paragraph of his press release:

'Announcing his decision, Mr Bowis today said: "No law can prevent the unforeseen disaster, but the law can ensure that the foreseeable is known to the public."'

This gives the author of the press release the opportunity to say his or her piece and explain the whole case behind the press release and its opening announcement. Note that a press release is always written in the third person; apart from your direct quotes never use terms such as 'I' or 'me'.

Getting it right

Let us return to the imaginary flower shop that is due to open up in the High Street of the equally imaginary Rossbury. Our florist, Veronica Green, has decided to celebrate the opening of her new shop by making a floral sculpture of Rossbury Castle, and has arranged for the Mayor to present it as a gift to the children's ward of the local hospital. Her press release might look something like this:

GREEN'S THE FLORIST

**27 High Street
Rossbury
Nr Easthampton
Leighshire, EH4 2FL
Tel: Easthampton 654321**

PRESS RELEASE: FOR IMMEDIATE RELEASE   **14th April 1993**

MAYOR HANDS OVER CASTLE TO SICK CHILDREN

The Mayor of Easthampton, Councillor Lizzy White, will next week present a massive floral sculpture of Rossbury Castle to patients in the children's ward at Easthampton General Hospital.

The 1.5-metre-high sculpture is being donated to the hospital by Veronica Green who recently opened a flower shop in Rossbury High Street - the first in the area.

Ms Green said today: 'Florists provide a very valuable service to the community and often at very difficult times. I am delighted to have opened shop in the town, and look forward to providing a comprehensive floral service to the people of Rossbury.'

She continued: 'As much of my work will be for visitors and patients at the hospital I thought it would be fun to create something special for the children's ward, and I am delighted that the Mayor is able to come along to present the sculpture.'

ENDS

NOTE FOR EDITOR: The floral sculpture will be collected from Green's by the Mayoral limousine at 2.30pm on Wednesday 21st April 1993 and transported to Easthampton General Hospital for a 3.00pm presentation.

FOR FURTHER INFORMATION: Veronica Green, Easthampton 654321

Veronica's press release opens with a paragraph which includes the four key 'W's:

- **Who** (Mayor of Easthampton)

- **What** (presents sculpture)

- **Where** (children's ward)

- **When** (next Wednesday afternoon)

Paragraph two outlines the reasons why; and this is amplified in her quotes in the third paragraph. Veronica then adds a footnote informing the editor of the details of the timing of this event. The release then ends with Veronica's phone number so that if journalists need any further information then she is only a phone call away.

However, in the introduction we saw that 'news' normally has three essential ingredients:

- **Human interest**

- **Topicality**

- **Conflict**

Veronica's event has the minimum two – human interest and topicality – but there is no conflict. This doesn't matter in this case as the originality of Veronica's scheme, and the Mayor's participation, gives the event a good chance of being reported in the local newspaper and radio station and, possibly, in the television station's news and magazine programmes.

However, all is not well in Rossbury, as down the road on the Whiteoak housing estate the residents have just learned that the government is looking at the option of building a motorway extension through part of the estate. The residents are up in arms, and are demanding that the council and local Member of Parliament oppose the plan, and help the residents find out how advanced or definite the plans may be. They have formed the Whiteoak Action Campaign and are planning a public meeting. Civil disobedience could follow if the plans get the go-ahead. The press release could read:

GARY BYSOUTH
7 Newcombe Close
Whiteoak Estate
Easthampton
EH2 9LU

PRESS RELEASE++PRESS RELEASE++PRESS RELEASE++PRESS RELEASE

FOR IMMEDIATE RELEASE   18th April 1993

RESIDENTS FIGHT MOTORWAY MADNESS

Government plans to build an extension of the M90
motorway through the outskirts of Easthampton are being
vigorously opposed by local residents who have pledged a
campaign of civil disobedience if the controversial scheme
gets the go-ahead.

The residents of the Whiteoak Estate on the north-east
edge of the town have called upon Easthampton District
Council and local Member of Parliament Sir William Bufton
to back their campaign and to press the Department of the
Environment to find an alternative route.

Local resident Gary Bysouth said: "It's disgusting to
think that the planners can propose such a devastating
scheme without even consulting local people. We must do
everything possible to protect our homes – even if it
means chaining ourselves to tractors and digger."

A public meeting has been organized for Friday 23rd
April 1993 at the St James Church Hall in Manor Road, and
will start at 7.00 p.m. The meeting will be chaired by
ward councillor Matthew Black, and Councillor Coral Gules,
Chair of Easthampton council's Planning Committee, has
been invited to attend.

                         E N D S

FOR FURTHER INFORMATION:
Gary Bysouth, Campaign Co-ordinator, Easthampton 789123
(evenings/weekends)

This press release says it all. Human interest, topicality and conflict are all there. It provides sufficiently detailed information – the name of the motorway and housing estate, the identity of the enemy, and the date and location of the public meeting. The one quote that is given clearly sums up the severity of the issue and the mood of the residents. We also read that a local councillor will be chairing the public meeting; that a council committee chairperson has been invited to the meeting; and that the local MP and council have been lobbied to oppose the development. All this is condensed into five sentences of around 170 words on one sheet of paper. If this was a real press release then the meeting on 23 April should be very well attended by representatives of the local newspapers, radio stations and television stations. And note that the press release is produced very simply on a manual typewriter.

Oh dear . . . not quite right

Compare the press release just described with the press release overleaf. The latter has a definite style problem and fails to grab the reader's attention in the first paragraph. Phrases such as 'Potent visual metaphors are employed by the artists as a means of exploring the behavioural patterns surrounding political struggle and loss' will need to be rewritten before they can be used by a journalist. Also, the press release is not on headed notepaper; there is no clear headline that instantly explains the nature of the story; the opening does little to grab the reader's attention; and the layout is not structured to work well as a press release.

:PRESS RELEASE:PRESS RELEASE:PRESS RELEASE:PRESS RELEASE:PRESS RELEASE:PRESSREL

FOR IMMEDIATE PUBLICATION   (VISUAL ART / PERFORMANCE / LESBIAN AND GAY)

NICHOLAS LOWE AND TIM BRENNAN ARE TO PRESENT A SITE SPECIFIC LIVE WORK AT THE
DIORAMA IN ASSOCIATION WITH THE AIDS COALITION TO UNLEASH POWER ACT UP AND THE
ORGANISATION FOR LESBIAN AND GAY ACTION OLGA.

THE WORK IS SCHEDULED TO BEGIN ON THE 17TH OF JANUARY 1990 AND WILL CONTINUE
UNTILLTHE 21ST OF JANUARY 1990. THE WORK WILL BE OPEN TO THE PUBLIC EACH DAY
BETWEEN 10:00A.M. AND 6:00P.M. FOR FURTHER DETAILS CONTACT THE DIORAMA ON 487 2896.
(DIORAMA, 14 PETO PLACE, LONDON, NW1.)

" INTERSTICE " is a four day live work located in the area between the outer wall
of the diorama and the main building. Potent visual metaphors are employed by the
artists as a means of exploring the behavioural patterns surrounding political
struggle and loss.

This event is the first official collaboration of these two artists. Their actions
are becoming increasingly noted for being part of the cutting edge of the visual arts.

TIM BRENNAN is a postgraduate student at the Slade school of art where he is
completeing research in fine art (Media). He is best known for his live works
which have been shown in this country and abroad. (Most notably the ICA last year)
Brennan has shown that his critical writing is essential to the development of his
arguments.

NICHOLAS LOWE has been making work in the discourse surrounding AIDS. His most
contoversial works were made at the Slade school as part of his research in fine
art (Media). Specifically the work ' (SAFE) SEX EXPLAINED ' can be seen at
Impressions gallery in York from the 27th of January to the 10th of March 1990,
as part of the touring exhibition ' EXSTATIC ANTIBODIES '.

Presentation

Although we have considered the content of a press release, the presentation of this central publicity document is of equal importance. There are a number of key points to be followed:

Headed notepaper

A press release should always be typed or word processed on A4-size paper – that is the standard size used in this country that measures 295 mm by 210 mm. Companies and other organizations will normally use their regular headed notepaper which is ideal for the purpose. Organizations who issue large quantities of press releases, such as major campaigning organizations, may consider having special press release headed notepaper printed by adapting the design of their headed notepaper. But for most of us such a luxury is too expensive. With the development of desk-top word processing facilities, many groups and individuals can produce very professional-looking documents. Check with local libraries or resource centres for details of facilities in your area. Even headed notepaper is not absolutely necessary, as the residents of the Whiteoak Estate demonstrated (see page 36). A sheet of white A4 paper and a manual typewriter can produce a very effective press release.

Embargo

Each of the press releases we have looked at so far have the phrase 'for immediate release' printed on the top left-hand side of the document. This simply tells the journalists that the story can be used straight away, and that it is up to the newspaper or broadcaster to decide which day the item is used. The alternative is the use of the embargo, when the producer of a press release can stipulate the date and time from which the item can be used.

An embargo is only used when the news contained in the press release is time-specific. For example, it might be strategically useful to the Whiteoak Estate Campaign to issue a press release announcing the next stage of their campaign to coincide with the next meeting of the council's Planning Committee – especially if they are planning highly visual publicity events, such as a picket of the meeting or perhaps a mock funeral (see Chapter 7). Such activities will add to the intensity of the campaign by focusing on the topicality and conflict values of their news. However, the journalists, photographers, sound recordists, camera operators, interviewers and editors will need to know about the event well in advance so they can organize coverage.

Let's say that the Planning Committee meeting is due to take place on Friday 30 April 1993. The Whiteoak Action Campaign decided on its campaign tactics at its meeting the previous week, and can issue a press release straight away marked 'Embargoed 00.01 30 April 1993'. The media people will receive copies of the press release on the Monday, or possibly Tuesday morning, and will have several days to arrange coverage of the Friday evening event. The '00.01' after the word 'embargo' means one minute past midnight. In other words the journalists are being told that they can run this story any time from Friday morning. The campaign will have decided that this will usefully put pressure on the councillors in advance of the meeting. Bear in mind that there is no legal requirement for journalists to honour an embargo instruction, and the embargo system has been abused by public relations bodies to manipulate the news. Only use an embargo to provide genuine advance notice to journalists, and use them sparingly. For most press releases an embargo is not necessary.

Date
Naturally, every press release should be dated, and the date should be typed at the top of the release on the same line as the embargo/for immediate release instruction.

Headline
The headline should summarize the nature of the press release in as few words as possible to grab the journalist's attention. But it does not have to be a clever tabloid-style headline with *double entendres* or witty use of language. Keep it simple.

'Private ambulances opposed by hospital staff' and 'Residents fight motorway madness' are simple and effective headlines that convey a straightforward message. That is all that is needed. The headline should be typed in block capitals – and in bold, if produced on a word processor – to make it stand out.

Margins

The press release should be typed with a margin of at least one inch, or 25 mm, down each side. This not only gives the release a neat appearance, but also provides space for the journalist to make brief notes in the margin when telephoning for further information.

Typing

The text of the press release should be typed double spaced; thus providing a wide gap between the lines which allows the journalist or sub-editor to 'mark up' the copy ready for typesetting. This tip ties in with the earlier advice on doing the journalists' job for them – do anything you can to help. Double spacing the text helps.

Indenting

The first line of each paragraph of the press release should be indented by three or four spaces. This is because the press release will be typed with double spacing between the lines throughout the text, and without the indentations we would not know where each paragraph ends and the next begins.

Continuation sheet

If your press release goes over to a second page then the letters 'm.f.' should be typed in the centre of the bottom of the first page. This simply means 'more follows' and informs the journalist that there is a continuation sheet. The top right-hand corner of the continuation sheet should contain a catchline and page number. The catchline is a word from the headline that links the second page with the first – such as 'Motorway' or 'Ambulance' or whatever is appropriate. Always ensure that any continuation sheet is marked clearly.

Ends

The word 'ends' should be typed at the end of the text used in the press release. This, of course, tells the journalist that the press release has come to an end. But it also indicates that any information that follows this point is not for publication or broadcast.

For further information

After the 'ends' tag always provide a contact name and telephone number so that journalists can telephone for further information or comments if necessary. Do state whether the contact numbers are home or work numbers – give both if possible. It is, of course, quite acceptable to give the names and telephone numbers of more than one contact.

Dispatch

Once your press release is completed then you will need sufficient copies for your hit-list of newspapers, radio and television stations (see Chapter 4). These can either be photocopied or the correct number can be printed on a word processor. If the press release is more than one page long then it should be stapled once in the very top left hand corner. This can then be sent without a covering letter to the news editor of each media organization on your list. Ideally the press release should be posted in an envelope of the same size so that it does not have to be folded. Alternatively, use an envelope that is 230 mm x 162 mm (9 in x 6½ in) so that the release only needs to be folded once. Access to a fax machine will clearly speed up the dispatch of a press release, but do also send out copies of the 'hard' copy as the quality will be superior and therefore appreciated by the reporters.

Types of press release

So far we have seen that press releases are used to inform the news desks of various media organizations about a news-worthy event that is due to take place; the vast majority of press releases are used for this straightforward purpose. But there are other occasions when a press release can be used:

Backgrounder

As we see in Chapter 3 a backgrounder is a detailed document – or series of documents – intended to brief journalists on particularly complex or detailed subjects. The backgrounder will be sent out with a covering press release, and in terms of presentation it follows all the rules of the press release.

Statement

Many of us will have seen television news programmes which show a written statement issued by Buckingham Palace or a celebrity. It is normally a short statement of only one or two paragraphs that makes a clear statement on a specific subject or event. Normally it is only royalty or celebrities who need to issue such statements, but it is also a tactic used by lawyers when a client has something public to say about a particular subject. As it takes a similar form to a news press release the statement is in writing and can be thoroughly checked before use. The statement is also put firmly on the public record, but is a rare event at a local level.

Photo-opportunity

Some events may only be visual, such as Greenpeace protesters scaling Big Ben or Nelson's Column. In such cases a very short press release announcing the who-what-where-when of the event can be sent to the news desk.

Text of a letter

Some issues of public importance may be confined to one person sending a letter to another person. For example, if a citizen has a complaint about the local council and wishes to report the council to the Local Government Ombudsman, then they have to do so in writing. Rather than producing a press release that may repeat all the points made in the letter, a copy of the letter can simply be press released. The covering release simply states that the attached letter has today been sent to the Ombudsman. It is normally a perfectly acceptable process for you to release copies of official letters to the press if they say something particularly important. But avoid doing so if the activity in which you are involved is likely to become a legal case, as such publicity might be damaging to your legal position.

Text of a speech

If a prominent person is to make an important speech, then the text of that speech can be circulated to the press and broadcast media in advance. This is the ideal time to use the embargo mechanism; the advance circulation gives the journalists time to read and digest the speech, and prepare their articles or broadcast scripts. But the embargo prevents them from reporting the speech until it is delivered. This could, for example, be useful to a councillor who is going to make a controversial statement at a council meeting and wants to alert the press in advance.

Feature article

You may wish to put your case by writing a feature article for a newspaper. A feature is an article of anything between 400 and 2000 words in length. In the national press an average feature article will be between 800 and 1000 words; in a local newspaper it will be less – maybe between 600 and 800 words.

The feature has a number of advantages: it helps the editor fill the pages of his or her newspaper; it provides information, and is therefore useful to the public; it can be billed as a 'comment' piece which is editorially independent from the newspaper. The main disadvantage is that a lot of work can be wasted by writing feature articles that are not used, so it is essential that you write an 'ideas' letter to the editor first to gauge the likelihood of your feature being accepted. Only put such a proposal forward if you feel confident that you can write to a high enough standard for a newspaper.

Other handy hints on writing feature articles: study your chosen newspaper in detail to assess the average length of its feature articles; use the press release style as the way to present your manuscript for easy editing purposes; if possible write your article on a word processor so that it can be read through and edited to a high standard before submitting it to the editor. As far as the finer skills of feature writing are concerned, there are numerous books on the market that offer advice and guidance on feature writing, and these may be available in public libraries or otherwise can be bought quite cheaply from bookshops. Two of the best books available are: *Teach Yourself Creative Writing* by Dianne Doubtfire (Hodder and Stoughton); and *The Art of Writing Made Simple* by Geoffrey Ashe (Heinemann).

How to get publicity for free – press release checklist

- A press release will need to contain at least two of the three essential news ingredients: human interest; topicality; and conflict.
- Keep the press release as short and simple as possible, and ensure that the opening paragraph contains the who-what-where-when details.
- Elaborate on those details in the second paragraph if necessary; otherwise go straight into the 'why' factors.
- When explaining 'why' the events in the first paragraph are taking place always quote directly from an individual who represents the organization.
- Follow the standard layout requirements of a press release as this helps the journalists use your story.
- Always provide a contact name and telephone number.
- Always check and re-check your facts.

3

Backgrounders

A backgrounder is an information sheet filled with a range of relevant facts about the topic contained in the press release. It pre-empts the questions that will come into the journalist's mind as soon as she has read the press release. Essentially, the press release is a sketch outline of the news story written in journalistic style that contains information on the who, what, where, when and why of the subject. The backgrounder then fills in the gaps: facts; figures; statistics; arguments; counter-arguments; dates; future plans; biographical details; additional quotes.

The material normally put into a backgrounder will be one of three types:

- Existing publicity material, such as a promotional leaflet, adapted as a backgrounder – perhaps by being neatly photocopied on to A4 paper and attached to the press release.

- A two- or three-page document, specifically prepared for the purpose, made up of several paragraphs – one on each area of additional information.

- A detailed series of already written briefings – background notes produced at an earlier stage for other purposes – that can be readily used to explain complex and technical subjects to journalists.

A backgrounder is by no means a necessary or essential addition to a press release; indeed, few press releases received by journalists will have this extra information attached. It is simply an additional tool that the publicist can use to increase further the probability of media coverage of an issue or event. Not all press releases need a backgrounder; it is entirely up to the originator of the press release to decide if the subject is sufficiently complex to require one.

One obvious question that can be raised about backgrounders is this: why not just produce a longer and more detailed press release? The answer: psychology. By producing a press release and a backgrounder, you are producing two separate and distinct documents. The first will be very familiar to the journalist, and will present information that can be used immediately by the reporter in the production of a news story. The backgrounder will be a less familiar document – but normally a very welcome one. As we have already seen, the role of the backgrounder is to pre-empt the journalist's follow-up questions. If the two documents were combined into one, then it would effectively require the publicist to write the entire news article. Few publicists will be skilled journalists and, in any event, it is the task of the journalist to write the article to the required length and in the style of that particular media organization. The role of the publicist is to provide the journalist with the necessary information so that he or she can do that job.

Making use of existing publicity material

The first type of backgrounder listed above is quite straightforward. A local branch of a national organization, for example, could simply copy a national leaflet or document that sets out the aims, objectives and activities of the organization. If this type of material is used then it should be presented on the same size paper (A4) as the covering press release. However, campaigning material comes in all shapes and sizes, so the simple solution when dealing with odd sizes is to photocopy it on to A4 paper.

Preparing a simple backgrounder

The most common type of backgrounder is the second in the list on page 46 – the two- or three-page backgrounder that is tailor-made for the press release to which it will be attached. Let us go back to Gary Bysouth's campaign to protest about the route of a proposed extension of the M90 motorway which may run through the Whiteoak Estate. Gary will need to prepare a specific backgrounder to accompany his model press release. But as soon as a journalist reads Gary's press release, the following questions will probably arise:

- How certain are the plans?

- What is the exact route of the proposed extension?

- Are there any alternative routes?

- When will it be built?

- How much will it cost?

- How many houses on the estate will be affected?

- How big is the estate?

- How many residents?

- When was it built?

- What is the council's policy/view of the plan?

- What is the campaign's plan of action?

- Who is behind the campaign?

- What broader support does the campaign have?

It is not a difficult task to anticipate many of the questions that the press and broadcast media might ask after reading a press release. Another advantage of using a backgrounder is that it further does the job of the journalist. Remember that the less work the journalist has to do on a story, the greater is the chance of that story appearing in print or on the airwaves.

As Gary has now drafted his list of probable questions, he can plan his backgrounder. He is aiming to confine it to two sides of A4 paper – maybe three – and draws up a rough outline of the paragraphs which may look something like this:

- **Introduction:** the first paragraph briefly introduces the subject of the backgrounder, and explains that it ties in with the press release to which it is attached.

- **The plans:** this part of the backgrounder will state how the local residents got to hear about the motorway extension plans in the first place, and will outline the precise information that they have in their possession at this stage.

- **The residents' views:** in this section the campaign will stress that they are not completely opposed to an extension of the motorway as they feel that it will ease the volume of traffic that runs through the town. But they are worried about the effect on their homes, and have counter-proposals that suggest an alternative route that will be less damaging to the community.

- **The campaign:** the next paragraph outlines the various campaign initiatives that the residents plan to take in order to oppose the motoway extension, including making contact with national pressure groups and lawyers that can advise them on various aspects of their campaigns.

- **The campaigners:** who is running the campaign? What do we know about Gary Bysouth? What is the background to Councillor Matthew Black? Who else is backing the campaign? The backgrounder reveals all.

- **Quotes:** the campaign's spokesperson, in this case Gary Bysouth, can provide additional quotes that are freely available to be used by the press in addition to those given in the press release.

With a little effort the backgrounder might look something like this:

GARY BYSOUTH
7 Newcombe Close
Whiteoak Estate
Easthampton
EH2 9LU

BACKGROUNDER++BACKGROUNDER++BACKGROUNDER++BACKGROUNDER++BACKGR

FOR IMMEDIATE RELEASE   18th April 1993

MOTORWAY MADNESS BACKGROUNDER

1. INTRODUCTION:

This Backgrounder is published in addition to the attached
Press Release dated 18th April 1993 and which is headed
"Residents Fight Motorway Madness". It is issued to provide
representatives of the press and broadcast media with
additional information on the Whiteoak Action Campaign, and
you are invited to use the information contained here in the
preparation of editorial material on the campaign.

2. THE PLANS:

The residents first became aware of plans to extend the M90
motorway when a local councillor, Matthew Black, received a
leaked copy of a council memorandum dated 2nd April 1993. The
memo was from the Chief Planning Officer to the council's
Chief Executive, and details Department of the Environment
plans to extend the M90 from Exit 17 to the junction of New
North Road and Manor Road to the south of the town. It will
then link up with the A907 dual carriageway and form a bypass
for much of the town's through traffic. The Whiteoak Action
Campaign has not seen a copy of the plans - only the leaked
memorandum. Neither the City Council nor the Department of the
Environment has been willing to discuss the scheme with
residents. It is believed that the plans as they stand will
require the demolition of at least twelve houses on the
estate. Whiteoak is made up of forty-eight houses and a total
of 144 residents.

3. THE RESIDENTS VIEW:

Residents on the Whiteoak Estate discussed the memorandum at a
meeting last week and accept that there is a problem with
traffic through the town at present, and that this is a
problem for motorists and pedestrians using the Manor Road -
including residents on the Whiteoak Estate. But they feel that
an extension of the motorway should run further eastward -
adjacent to the British Rail Rossbury Valley line. This would
prevent the demolition of any residential property, and keep
traffic noise and atmospheric pollution in the area to a
minimum.

m.f.

4. THE CAMPAIGN:

The Whiteoak Action Campaign has the backing of every
household on the estate, and will meet every Monday evening at
the St James' Church Hall at 7.00 p.m. Its first task is to
find out exactly how advanced the plans are, and lobby the
local council and local MP, Sir William Bufton, to oppose the
current plans. The campaign has contacted the Council for the
Protection of Rural England and the Town and Country Planning
Association to find out what professional help and advice is
available. The campaign is also consulting local community
lawyer Rebecca Seligman on what legal action might be taken to
obtain information and block the plans.

5. WHO'S WHO:

The residents last week elected Councillor Matthew Black as
Chair of the Whiteoak Action Campaign. He is a resident of the
estate and has lived there for the past nine years. Matthew
has been an independent councillor on Easthampton City Council
for four years, and works as a Charge Nurse at Easthampton
General Hospital.

The Campaign Co-ordinator, who will be organizing the
camnpaign's activities and acting as its press officer, is
Gary Bysouth who lives on the estate with his two children.
Gary, who works from home, is a freelance illustrator of
children's books.

The campaign's treasurer is local resident Jonathan Q. Jones,
who is a Chartered Accountant with an advertising agency in
Rosebury.

6. QUOTES:

Campaign Co-ordinator Gary Bysouth said today: "The most
frightening thing is the secrecy that surrounds these plans.
We only know about them because of a leaked memo. The
community should have the right to know what is going on in
their own back yard. We demand the right to be fully consulted
about such plans - and to put our objections and counter
proposals to the planners."

He continued: "The Whiteoak Action Campaign is supported by
every household on the estate. We will fight the development
to the end and will take whatever action is necessary to get
through to these bureaucrats. We trust that we will be fully
backed by the local council and MP. That's what they are there
for, and local people can expect their elected representatives
to pull out all the stops when a crisis like this arises. We
look forward to their support."

E N D S

This backgrounder provides journalists with ample information about the range of issues thrown up by the revelation of the motorway extension plans. But it also paves the way for the campaign to receive substantial follow-up media coverage in the weeks and months following the launch of the campaign. This is because it raises a number of important issues that will not be resolved by the time the first news items appear. The outstanding matters are:

- **The local Member of Parliament:** the local MP, Sir William Bufton, has been approached by the campaign but has yet to respond to their calls for help and support. Before the MP gives any response he will need to find out for himself exactly what the Department of the Environment is planning. This will take several days – or even a week or two – and the local journalists will therefore need to follow up Sir William's position on this controversial development.

- **The City Council:** the Whiteoak Estate Campaign has also lobbied the council for help opposing the motorway extension. Most local government authorities operate their meetings on a six-weekly cycle and so it may well be several weeks before the council develops a clear and coherent position on the plans.

- **Pressure groups:** two national pressure groups have been approached by the campaign for specialist advice and assistance. They are the Council for the Protection of Rural England, and the Town and Country Planning Association. The advice that eventually comes from these groups can be drip-fed to the media as it suits the campaign.

- **Legal advice:** will the campaign go to court to prevent the development from going ahead? Can they insist upon a planning inquiry to debate the proposals and counter-proposals? What Freedom of

Information laws exist that can be used to force the council to reveal information? And so on. Each of these questions begs an answer, and each answer will be a news story in itself.

Therefore the campaign is in a position to create its own media campaign around the gradual developments that will take place on the motorway extension. Each week it could ensure that one major news story breaks in the local media about the plan. For example, in between announcements about the position of the Member of Parliament and the city council, the campaign could gradually release developments on the advice it has received from its lawyers; on the growth of support for the campaign from elsewhere in the town; fundraising events; and similar issues.

In this example it is likely that Gary Bysouth would receive several calls each week from journalists enquiring about the latest developments on this story – all because he was prepared to invest a few hours in producing a good press release and thorough backgrounder.

Another spin-off that can arise from providing the media with detailed briefing material of this type are feature articles – or features as they are better known – and personality profiles of the leading figures behind the campaign. Such material is even more time-consuming for the journalists to write than news items; once again, if you hand the information to them on a plate, and even the idea that they should write a feature or other background article, then your publicity campaign is likely to go far.

Press packs

Although Gary Bysouth provided the media with quite detailed background information in his backgrounder, the document was eventually only two pages long. Some issues, however, will be so technical or so complex that they will require detailed press packs in order to provide journalists and editors with all the relevant background information. This could apply to scientific issues; industrial processes; medical breakthroughs; legal cases; and such like.

One clear example of the effective use of detailed briefing material for journalists was a legal campaign in the mid-1980s involving a raid on a gay bookshop in London by officers from Her Majesty's Customs and Excise. The bookshop, Gay's The Word, in Bloomsbury's Marchmont Street, is the biggest lesbian and gay bookshop in Europe and stocks a wide range of literature. In October of 1984 the bookshop was raided by officers from Customs and Excise who seized thousands of copies of some 142 titles under the obscure Customs Consolidation Act of 1876. Customs and Excise took an interest in the bookshop because it imported much of its stock from a supplier in the United States, and such stock therefore came within the scope of customs law. Many of the titles seized in the raid – including work by such distinguished authors as Gore Vidal, Jean Genet, Edmund White and Tennessee Williams – had been quite legally published in this country. However, the authorities considered that it was illegal to *import* the same titles into the UK because of a major quirk in the obscenity laws. It was widely believed at the time that the government was using this discrepancy in the law to launch an unwarranted and vindictive attack on the lesbian and gay communities.

Following the raid a major defence campaign was launched, and it attracted the support of MPs, publishers, trade unions, journalists, booksellers, civil rights campaigners, authors, lawyers and many ordinary women and men concerned about the obvious censorship implications of the case. With a trial due to take place at the Old Bailey, the Gay's The Word case was poised to become the most controversial censorship case since the *Lady Chatterley's Lover* case in 1960. Instead, though, only weeks before the trial was due to take place, Her Majesty's Customs and Excise withdrew the charges in a humiliating and very public retreat.

The campaign had been a stunning success. But consider the complexities of communicating all the appropriate information to the press and broadcast media: the original raid; the titles and number of books seized; the bookshop's background; the complexities of the law; the anti-censorship arguments; details of the campaign and its wide body of support; and the future.

This was therefore the ideal case for a series of backgrounders to be published together in a press pack. Each backgrounder will cover a separate theme and spell out in simple terms the facts of the case and the arguments that the campaign wants to communicate to the media and the public at large.

The resulting press pack was made up as follows:

- **Press release:** the first document in the press pack was the formula press release giving details of who, what, where, when – and then why. The press release opened:

  '*A controversial censorship case against a leading gay and lesbian bookshop which was to be heard at the Old Bailey next month crashed dramatically today following the withdrawal of criminal charges by Her Majesty's Customs and Excise.*'

  It then went on to explain the reasons for the withdrawal of the charges and then quoted both the bookshop manager and campaign worker on the victory. This press release covered two sides of A4 paper.

- **Backgrounder 1:** this document was entitled 'A Short History' and provided precisely that, on both the bookshop itself and on the raid and seizure of the books. The five paragraphs were headed: Gay's The Word; The Raids; Seizures and Charges; Committal Hearing; and The Campaign. This document also covered two sides of A4.

- **Backgrounder 2:** at this stage it was appropriate to list the 142 titles that had been seized by Customs and Excise and then returned to the shop when the

charges were dropped. Although this backgrounder
only had a brief one-paragraph introduction it
extended to a total of four sides of A4 because of the
volume of books seized. It was simply headed 'The
Books'.

- **Backgrounder 3:** the third backgrounder was headed
'The Law' and outlined the legal issues in this case.
This included a statement on the Act of Parliament
used by Customs and Excise, the Customs
Consolidation Act of 1876, and contrasted it with the
Obscene Publications Act 1959 which regulates the
publication of literature in the United Kingdom. It
also mentioned that the 1876 Act originated because
of a scandal that hit Victorian England when
indecent chess pieces imported from France were
discovered in a girls boarding school in Kent.
Journalists like a laugh, and this type of anecdote
adds to the human interest content of the news item.
This backgrounder covered two pages.

- **Backgrounder 4:** this document was entitled 'The
Campaign' and set out to explain the arguments
against the seizures and in favour of the right to
distribute the titles: that the law on material
published here conflicted with the law on that
imported from abroad; that the books seized were
works of literature and not pornography; that adults
should have the freedom to choose what they read;
that there were no victims as a result of those titles
being imported – except for the directors of the
bookshop. This was effectively a 'soapbox'
backgrounder that gave the campaign the
opportunity to put its case to the media. This
document extended to three sides of A4.

- **Backgrounder 5:** 'The Future'. The campaign had
been a success, but it did not come to an end with
the withdrawal of the charges. There was more work

to do: the result of the campaign needed to be documented and published for future reference; pressure needed to continue to be put upon the politicians to change the law; the directors, and the bookshop itself, needed to pick up the pieces and plan their futures. All this information needed to be communicated to the world, and so the three pages of backgrounder number five was an effective way of outlining those future plans.

The press pack totalled sixteen pages of easily digestible facts, figures and quotes about a complex legal issue. The recipient journalists greatly appreciated this information being presented in a highly usable format. Indeed, this story hit the front page of the *Guardian* the next day, and received widespread media attention involving dozens of press articles and radio interviews.

The following guidelines may help in ensuring that the press pack is well presented.

- If you have headed notepaper, then use it for the first page of each backgrounder. Ensure that the headline clearly states the subject matter of that particular backgrounder. The backgrounders can be individually numbered if the order is important or if an index is used.

- Do not staple all of the backgrounders together, but do ensure that the sheets of each one are firmly stapled together with one staple in the top left-hand corner.

- The top document of the press pack will be the press release – there is no need for a covering document. However, if the press pack consists of more than two or three backgrounders then an index can be produced. This should be printed or typed on a single sheet of headed notepaper and placed between the press release and the first backgrounder.

● To keep all this material neatly together it is a good idea to send the press pack out in clear plastic A4 wallets that can be bought cheaply at most stationery shops.

How to get publicity for free – backgrounder checklist

● Remember the key publicity maxim – the more reseach you do for the journalists then the greater are the chances of your press releases and backgrounders being used.
● Anticipate the questions that will be raised by the journalists once they have read the press release. Provide them with the answers in the backgrounder.
● When compiling a press pack give each back-grounder a specific task and confine the information in that document to that particular aspect of your subject.
● Presentation is very important. Ensure that the press release and backgrounder are in the appropriate order and held together in a plastic A4 wallet.

4

Contacting the media

Once the press release has been written and copied – with the backgrounder, if one is to be used – it will be necessary to draw up a distribution list of newspapers, radio stations and television stations to whom the release will be sent. Of course, there is no obligation on any publicist to send a copy of a press release to every media organization in the area; you can be as selective as you wish. But most publicity campaigns will operate along the lines that 'all publicity is good publicity' and produce a comprehensive distribution list for its area.

Where is the media?

To draw up a distribution list it will be necessary to identify the local and regional media and find out where they are located. There are several ways to get this information:

Personal knowledge
Most people will have some idea of which newspapers, radio stations and television channels serve their community. Friends, neighbours and colleagues will no doubt be able to provide valuable advice on this matter.

Local newspapers
The easiest way to find out which newspapers serve your area is to call in at your local newsagent and take a look. The local

library will probably stock copies of all local newspapers (and often back-issues) for public reference.

Radio and television stations

It is most likely that all programmes on the local radio and television stations will be listed in the local newspapers. The addresses, however, might not be listed. So look under 'Broadcasting organizations' in the *Yellow Pages*. All areas of the UK are served by one regional television service of the BBC which slots into the BBC1 broadcast schedules, and one regional independent television station – in addition to BBC2 and Channel 4. Similarly, most areas of the country are served by one local BBC radio station and at least one local independent radio station.

News agencies

Your area may be served by freelance journalists or a news agency that cover stories for the local press and which also act as contacts for the national newspapers. Be sure to include them on your mailing list. Check under 'News and photo agencies' and 'Journalists' in the *Yellow Pages*.

Specialist press

The specialist press are newspapers and, more often, magazines and newsletters that specialize in a particular subject. A glance at the shelves of a well-stocked newsagent's will show that there are endless specialist titles covering popular subjects, such as personal computers, photography and fashion. In fact, there are more than 9000 such periodicals in the UK, covering every conceivable subject. You may be able to rely on your own personal knowledge of the subject area; otherwise consult the various press and media directories that list such titles (see Directories, opposite page). Then add the appropriate titles to your mailing list.

A small proportion of specialist periodicals are not available for the public to buy in newsagents' as they are posted directly to their intended audience. For example, the medical magazine *Pulse* is mailed out directly to general medical practitioners – it cannot be bought by anybody else. Similarly, the trade union magazine *Public Service* is distributed directly to members of the trade union NALGO. However, press releases can be targeted to restricted-circulation magazines in exactly the same way as for other media organizations.

Bear in mind that there may be specialist television and radio programmes that cover the subject area that you are dealing with. For example, BBC Radio 4 puts out specialist programmes on farming (*Farming Today*); law (*Law in Action*); science (*Science Now*); etc. Check the broadcasting listings to see if there is an appropriate programme covering your area of activity and, if so, direct your press release impersonally to the producer of the programme.

Directories

There are two main media directories which detail information about newspapers and the broadcast media: *Willings Press Guide* and *Benns Media Directory*. These are often stocked by local reference libraries. The *Willings Press Guide* only covers newspapers and magazines; *Benns Media Directory* covers the entire media industry. Even if the local reference library does not stock these titles, it should have detailed information on all media organizations that serve the area.

To gauge how a media list will be put together, let us look at the media organizations that serve three very different communities in the UK:

TOTNES

Totnes is a small town in Devon midway between Exeter and Plymouth. It is served by one regional daily newspaper; three local newspapers; two television channels; one BBC local radio station; and three independent radio stations. They are:

- *Western Morning News* (paid-for daily newspaper; circulation approximately 60,000).

- *Totnes Times Gazette* (paid-for weekly newspaper; circulation approximately 19,000)

- *Totnes Weekender* (free-distribution weekly newspaper; circulation approximately 68,000 throughout the county).

- *Totnes News-Shopper* (free-distribution weekly newspaper; circulation approximately 14,800).

- *BBC South-West* (BBC regional television centre based in Plymouth).

- *Westcountry Television* (regional independent television channel based in Plymouth).

- *BBC Radio Devon* (local county-wide station with studios in Plymouth and Exeter).

- *Plymouth Sound* (independent local radio station).

- *DevonAir Radio* (independent local radio station).

- *South West 103* (independent local radio station).

MANCHESTER

Manchester is not only a major northern city but is also the provincial centre for the north-west of England. Its main media organizations are:

- *Manchester Evening News* (paid-for daily newspaper; circulation approximately 267,000).

- *East Manchester Reporter* (paid-for weekly newspaper; circulation approximately 33,000).

- *Twelve Free Weekly Newspapers* (each serving a particular part of the city and surrounding districts).

- *BBC North* (BBC regional television centre).

- *Granada Television* (regional independent television channel).

- *Radio GMR* (BBC local radio station).

- *Key 103* (independent local radio station).

- *Piccadilly Gold* (independent local radio station).

- *Sunset Radio* (independent local radio station).

BRIGHTON

Brighton is a large town on the south coast of England which is a popular tourist resort for both native and overseas visitors. The media outlets in Brighton are:

- *Evening Argus* (paid-for daily newspaper; circulation approximately 88,500).

- *Brighton and Hove Leader* (free weekly newspaper; circulation approximately 133,000).

- *BBC Television* (regional programmes based at Elstree).

- *TVS* (regional independent television channel with studio facilities in Brighton).

- *BBC Radio Sussex* (local county-wide BBC station).

- *Southern Sound FM* (independent local radio station).

- *South Coast Radio* (independent local radio station).

Therefore, Brighton has access to seven local media outlets; Manchester has twenty; and Totnes has ten. Some towns may have as few as four such outlets: two regional television channels; one BBC local radio station; and one local newspaper. Major cities – such as London or Edinburgh – will be served by a seemingly endless range of media organizations, in which case the publicist will need to decide which to include on the media mailing list. Even in Manchester, with its twenty or so newspapers, radio stations and television channels, a press release mailing will cost approximately £10 – bearing in mind that each press release will cost around 50p to produce and send out. If this is too expensive then the publicist may decide not to include the twelve free-distribution newspapers on the mailing list. The cost of the mailing could then be reduced to £4. But beware! Do not automatically ignore the free-distribution newspapers as some have huge circulation figures. The *Brighton and Hove Leader*, for example, has a weekly circulation of some 133,000 copies. Such newspapers may also have only one journalist writing all of the news stories. Remember the maxim of doing the journalist's job for her. Once all the information about local media outlets has been collated it will be possible to produce a mailing list.

Each press release should be sent impersonally to the news editor and not to any named individual. As your relationship with the media develops you may establish regular contact with individual journalists and producers, and these can be added to the mailing list. It is, however, wise to keep the unnamed news editor on the list and invest in expanding the list as this will increase the attention that your press release receives.

If you are writing to a television station, add the name of the programme to your mailing list. Particularly important are news magazine programmes covering local and regional news. The magazine programmes are usually broadcast in the early evening at either 6.00 or 6.30 each weekday. They are incredibly popular and attract very high viewing figures. Even the country's smallest television station, Channel Television, in the Channel Islands, broadcasts a thirty-minute magazine programme each weekday evening – the only programme broadcast by the station that it makes itself! Most television channels also run news bulletins throughout the day, and they are all produced by the same team that make the early evening news magazine slot.

Chat shows

The structure of local radio is slightly different from that of television, and this will affect who you send your press releases to. As with television, there will be a news team that oversees the production of both the main news programmes as well as the on-the-hour bulletins. But many radio stations also broadcast programmes that invite local celebrities to come into the studio to be interviewed live. For example, on Greater London Radio (GLR), the BBC's popular London-wide station, some six hours of such programmes are broadcast each weekday, and this involves the interviewing of about thirty guests per week ('talking heads' as they are known in the business). Some are famous household names. Many are unknown, but have something important or interesting to say. Nearly all of them are invited to appear on the programme because either they, or someone acting on their behalf, has sent the programme producer a press release. Most areas of the country are served by at least one radio station providing that type of quality programming. There is absolutely nothing to lose by putting the producers of chat shows on your mailing list.

Community publications

There may also be other publications in your community to whom you should consider sending copies of the press release. They include parish magazines, student newspapers, ethnic-minority press and the many newsletters that are published by local community groups such as tenants' associations, gay groups, local branches of environmental pressure groups and so on. Never underestimate the benefits that can be achieved by mailing to newsletters with quite small circulations. For campaigning organizations and voluntary groups it might be just the way to enlist additional support or recruit new members. Don't forget to consider local listings magazines too, and other free-distribution 'what's on' publications that carry some local news. It is, of course, possible to include such fringe publications on a trial-and-error basis; if you receive no coverage or feedback from such titles then they can simply be deleted from the mailing list.

Speaking to journalists

Once the press release has been sent out it is likely that, if your story is to be used, you will receive a telephone call from the journalist. There are two reasons for this: firstly, the journalist will want to authenticate the story and its source, particularly if the organization or individual publishing the release is not known to the local media. It is not unknown for bogus press releases to be sent out to discredit organizations – particularly in the political and campaigning fields. The second reason, of course, is that the journalist may need additional information and quotes in order to produce an article.

The rules for conducting interviews with journalists are basically the same as for handling radio interviews (see Chapter 5). They can be summarized as:

● Remember that you are the expert on the subject of the interview, and once you have had some experience of dealing with journalists you will find that you can control the direction of the interview.

● If you are able and willing to give straight answers to straight questions then remember that you cannot withdraw an answer once it has been given. Give honest, factual answers that you know to be true. Otherwise avoid the question altogether.

● Remember, there is no law requiring you to answer a journalist's question. You are at liberty to answer the question in kind by repeating a few hard-hitting points that you consider to be important.

● Have your answers and/or hard-hitting points prepared in advance. The press release is a very brief statement of the main issues – it will not contain all of the issues or all of the facts and figures or all of the quotes. You are the source of that knowledge, and you can make the journalist's task that much easier by having all the necessary information at your fingertips.

Off the record

Unless you are dealing with a journalist who is a good personal friend, or you have had years of experience in handling the local media and know exactly how they operate, then the golden rule of speaking 'off the record' is straightforward – don't. Only ever say anything to a journalist that you would be prepared to see in print or hear broadcast across the airwaves. Of course, you can speak confidently about your subject in the knowledge that not every word you speak will be quoted; and, similarly, do speak in a relaxed and friendly manner. But beware of journalists attempting to prise an 'off the record' comment out of you.

There are two main hazards that may confront the budding publicist who is talked into speaking off the record. The first is that the conversation may not in fact be off the record at all. Although most journalists will conduct their work in an acceptable and ethical manner, the trade does have its unscrupulous elements and it will probably be impossible to disprove a subsequent claim that your statement was given on the record. The second hazard is that anything supposedly said off the record can be as libellous as any other type of comment – and by its very nature may well be more libellous. If the issue arises, simply inform the inquiring journalist that everything you have to say is strictly on the record, and then relay the facts and comments that you would happily see in print.

Some professional publicists do have proven techniques of speaking off the record, but they ensure that one key condition is fulfilled – that such a statement is only made in a face-to-face conversation where there are no witnesses and little chance of the conversation being recorded. An additional safeguard is to couch the conversation in very ambiguous terms, and imply that the information is third hand. For example, they may start the sentence by saying, 'It has been suggested that . . .' or 'You may not be entirely wrong to draw the conclusion that . . .' But this is the work of professional publicists who know that the participating journalist is playing the same game by the same rules.

How to get publicity for free – contacting the media checklist

- The media list. Draw up a media mailing list for your area that includes all local newspapers, radio stations and television channels. Mark each entry impersonally for the attention of the news editor.
- Tell the community. Include small, community-based publications such as parish magazines, campaign newsletters and 'What's On' listings magazines on your mailing list.
- Be my guest! Also send your press release to the producer of regional television magazine programmes and radio chat shows for additional coverage.
- Do your homework. Be prepared for questions from journalists by having appropriate information readily at hand. This could include statistical information; additional facts and figures; and opinions that can be given as quotes.
- Off the record. Never agree to speak to journalists 'off the record' – insist that all your conversations are on the record and attributable.

5

The radio interview

Radio is an expanding industry with many new stations going on air every year, and with many more planned for the future at both a local and national level. This applies to both the network of local and regional BBC stations and the variety of independent commercial stations that serve most communities around the UK. Radio is a very popular medium, and local stations often attract much larger audiences than local newspapers. Unlike television, however, there are numerous radio programmes that are hungry for news, features and personality interviews.

In terms of news and magazine programmes it is usually the local or regional BBC stations that give over air time for current affairs coverage. This is because they have the financial backing to allocate time and resources to provide such a service. Independent commercial radio stations, however, rely on advertising revenue for their income and have to aim for the highest possible audience figures. This means that their output is invariably made up of popular music and 'easy-listening' music programmes. Accordingly, the commercial stations do not have the staff or other resources to match the BBC stations, and they allocate relatively little transmission time to news bulletins – maybe four or five minutes per hour on average.

Many of the independent radio stations will rely on one or two journalists to research and produce their entire news output. Once again, the publicist is therefore provided with plenty of opportunities to do the journalist's job for him by handing a press release and backgrounder package to the hard-pressed hack.

The press release that goes out to the local radio stations is exactly the same as the one sent out to the newspapers – and that goes for backgrounders, if they are used. Unlike newspaper journalists, however, the radio journalists will normally either have to come to you – or invite you to go to them – for a face-to-face interview. As with newspaper interviews, some radio interviews are conducted over the telephone. This is quite a common interviewing technique, but do try to avoid telephone interviews if at all possible as they provide the lowest quality of speech reproduction.

Types of radio interview

Interviews can be conducted in a variety of ways, and there are basically six different types of radio interview.

Recorded on location
Most radio interviews for news and magazine programmes will be recorded on to tape in advance of transmission and then edited into shape by the reporter or producer. For an interview to be recorded on location a radio journalist will visit you, or attend your event, and bring a tape recorder with her. The interview is very immediate and happens on your territory, but the interview techniques are much the same whatever type of interview is conducted.

Recorded in the studio
Radio journalists are busy people and are likely to ask you to go into the studio for the interview to save time. Most radio interviews are studio recorded. If for some reason you are unable to agree to visit the studio, or you are unwilling to do so, then the journalist will probably ask you to give the interview over the telephone (see Telephone interviews, page 72).

Live on location

This is a relatively rare interviewing technique, especially for local radio stations. Live location interviews are usually conducted only for one of two reasons. Firstly, you are such an important person that the radio station wants a live interview wherever you happen to be – and regardless of cost. Few of us fall into the catagory of celebrity who is interviewed 'live from the radio car'; you need to be a high-ranking public figure to qualify for that privilege. The other time a radio car might be used is when the news is unable to travel to the studio – in the event of a disaster or a major public event that is highly newsworthy – and therefore needs the radio station to travel to it.

Live in studio

A guest may be invited to speak to a programme presenter live in the studio. In the case of news programmes this is rare, as the producer much prefers to have the interview recorded on to tape and then slotted into the programme. This has little, if anything, to do with censorship or the political manipulation of the news. On a radio news programme every second counts, and the producers will allocate your news item a slot of only three or four minutes, the average duration of a radio news item. In that short period of time the programme makers need to convey all of the appropriate facts and interview at least two people. This requires precision timing and cannot be left to chance. In most cases this will be to the publicist's benefit as any mistakes can be edited out, and the straightforward who, what, where, when and why information and opinion is included. It is only well-known local dignitaries such as a leading councillor or other news-maker who will be invited to give a live interview.

Down the line

This is a potentially difficult interview to undertake because you are in one part of the country or county, and the radio station wanting to interview you is somewhere else entirely. However, that station may have studio facilities elsewhere, such as in a conference centre or police headquarters, or may ask you to visit a sister station nearby. These interviews can be more difficult to participate in because you cannot see the interviewer and need to wear headphones for the interview to take place. However, by the time your cause attracts such widespread media interest that a down-the-line interview is required, the chances are that you will have done some studio or location interviews before, and will therefore be able to handle the experience.

Telephone interviews

It is quite commonplace for radio interviews to be conducted over the phone, but the quality of such interviews is not as good as when using studio facilities. Telephone interviews take place if it is not possible for you to get to the studio – or one of its reporters to get to you – in time for the transmission. This may be because you are nowhere near a radio studio, or because a story has just broken and the station wants your immediate response.

Alternatively, it might not be convenient for you to visit the station, as you may have work or child-care responsibilities. However, when doing a telephone interview do try to arrange it so that you will not be disturbed by the kids or the dog or the door bell.

Before the interview

Before an interview takes place the reporter or producer will have contacted you by telephone to arrange the interview. It is at this stage that you can ask what angle the interview will take, or you could simply ask what questions will be put to you. The vast majority of radio journalists and producers will want to make a straightforward news item without taking sides on the issue either way. They will want a hassle-free interview that makes good radio. Although they have no obligation to inform you of their intended questions, it is as much in their interest as yours to co-operate with you by discussing the questions in advance. Only when you appear live on agenda-setting news programmes like the BBC Radio 4 *Today* programme or *Any Questions?* will you encounter trick questions or manipulative interviewers.

Another important feature of preparation is to give yourself enough time to consider the issues and questions in advance of the interview. This will give you the chance to plan the responses you want to get across in the interview – both fact and opinion. If, though, a radio journalist calls you and wants to tape a telephone interview straight away you are well within your rights to ask her to call you back in, say, fifteen or twenty minutes' time so that you can prepare yourself. Do not forget that the publicist has the upper hand in these events because it is *your* news, and the media industry needs you as much as – if not more than – you need it.

You may want to have a written prompt in front of you to remind you of the four or five main points of your argument, and perhaps one or two key figures or statistics. Fine. But do take it from an experienced broadcaster that over-preparation does far more harm than good. Having too much information written down in front of you just clouds your mind and confuses you as soon as the interview begins. Use a 5 in x 3 in card or one page from a small notebook to note down those few points; after all, you are being interviewed because you are the expert on this topic, so make the most of your memory and expertise.

Perhaps our friend Gary Bysouth back in Easthampton is feeling a little apprehensive about his first-ever radio interview for the local station Radio LCR. He knows that the whole item will last approximately five minutes, and that his interview will fill little more than two minutes of that slot. He needs to be sure of the four or five main points he wants to get across in the interview. On a rough piece of paper he outlines those points:

1. There has been no consultation about the motorway proposals; we only know about the plan at all because of a leaked council memo.

2. Although the town needs a bypass this is not the most appropriate route to take as it will cause some houses to be demolished and blight the rest of the estate. And a better route would be along the railway line – less noise and air pollution.

3. When will there be consultation on the plans, or a public inquiry? Can we take any legal action?

4. We are calling upon our local MP and the council to fight the Department of the Environment plans. Also getting advice from the Council for the Protection of Rural England and the Town and Country Planning Association.

5. Facts and figures to remember for the interview: 48 houses with 144 residents; 12 houses may need to be demolished under these plans. Public meeting next *Friday, 23rd April*.

These notes outline the main points of Gary's interview, and will provide him with just the right amount of information for his two minutes. But they are still far too detailed for use in the studio because he will need to *read* the notes before he can use them, thus either killing the interview dead, or making it sound very wooden indeed. So those notes have to be cut right down to simple prompt points. They might look like this:

1. No consultation, only leaked memo.

2. We need a bypass – run extension along railway line?

3. What consultation? Public inquiry? Legal action.

4. Sir William Bufton MP – local council.

5. Council for the Protection of Rural England.
Town and Country Planning Association.
48 houses and 144 residents – 12 demolitions?
Meeting: Friday 23rd April, 7.00pm, St James's.

Therefore Gary will have before him a very concise and uncluttered series of pointers to guide him through the interview. They briefly state the main point of each key argument in a few words. The final pointer gives important names and numbers that Gary will not be able to carry around in his head with certainty. These will be listed in chronological order for easy reference.

Getting there

Give yourself more than enough time to get to the studio. If you do not have your own transport, and public transport is not available – maybe you are being asked to visit the studio at a particularly unsocial hour – then ask for the station to arrange a taxi. Whatever mode of transport you use, do try to arrive at the studio ten or fifteen minutes before the pre-arranged time. It is also important to dress smartly for the interview and check your appearance; obviously a radio audience cannot see a radio interviewee, but if you are smartly dressed you will feel better about yourself and the interviewer may well feel better about you. Dressing smartly will help your performance.

Nerves

Some people can simply walk into a radio studio, sit down in front of a microphone ten seconds before the interview, and deliver a perfect four-minute interview with considerable ease. Most cannot. Even the slickest performer will have memories of early interviews that he would prefer to forget. For many of us, participating in an interview on radio is a matter of trial and error; you can only learn by doing it.

Relax

One reason for arriving early at the studio is so that you can wait in the reception area and relax a little before going into the interview. This will allow you to catch your breath and let your heartbeat settle down. You may find it enough to sit quietly for a few minutes looking at your prompt notes or having another read through the press release. However, if

you feel particularly nervous try some deep-breathing
exercises: sit up straight, take a deep breath and hold it for
two seconds; let it out in a long, deep sigh whilst counting in
your mind backwards from eight to one. Try this exercise two
or three times. It can help you relax.

Dry mouth

Take along a small bottle of still mineral water with you to
the studio, as one common ailment during radio interviews is
dry mouth. There may be water in the studio for you to
drink, but often there is not. Even if water is provided there is
no way of telling the vintage. Take your own – you may need
it. Also, remember not to take mobile telephones, bleeps or
digital watches into the studio as they have the potential to
cause considerable disruption to a programme.

The studio

You will be met in reception by either the journalist who is to
conduct the interview, or a producer. As the interview will
probably be pre-recorded you will be shown to a simple studio
that will be away from the main broadcast studios – in the
basement or suchlike. This studio will be very unglamorous:
one table with two microphones positioned for interviews; two
seats on opposite sides of the table; and one very large tape
recorder located behind one of the seats.

Getting prepared

Once you are shown to your seat, put the prompt card and
your bottle of water on the table in front of you. That is all
you should need for the interview. You may have a minute
or so spare while the reporter sets up a tape on the tape
recorder. Use that time. Make yourself comfortable by sitting
with both feet on the floor; your back straight; both hands in
your lap. Perhaps you should do some more deep breathing.
Clear your throat and take a sip of water if you wish. Check
your prompt notes. You may find the interview a little easier
if you try to think of the interview as a discussion between
yourself, the interviewer and one listener. In a way that is

exactly what it is; think of it as a cosy chat between the three of you.

The interview

Style

Once you are prepared, and once the interviewer has prepared the tape recorder, the interview is ready to go ahead. The first thing to do is to establish eye contact with the interviewer. The interview is essentially a conversation between the two of you, and eye contact is an essential ingredient – as it is in any other type of conversation. Of course you can break eye contact any time you wish. Just try to act as normally and naturally as possible. Also, do remain calm and polite throughout the interview despite your feelings about the issue. Your audience will automatically feel hostile towards any stroppy character they hear on the radio and, equally, feel sympathetic towards a confident and polite interviewee – often irrespective of the subject. Some of the most marginal and controversial causes have been championed by polite campaigners who remain cool, calm and collected, in spite of any pressure put on them by interviewers.

Soundbites

The interview begins and you are asked the first question. How should you present your answers? Each answer should be given in what is called a soundbite. A soundbite is an answer of around twenty to thirty seconds which does three things: clearly states the problem or issue to which you are responding; gives you an opportunity to give your opinion of that point; and then leads you neatly into providing a solution to the original proposition. Thus, suppose Gary Bysouth is sitting in the studio at Radio LCR and the first question put to him is this:

'*Gary Bysouth. You are the co-ordinator of the Whiteoak Action Campaign. Why are you opposed to an extension of the M90 motorway?*'

He glances at his first prompt point which reads: 'No consultation, only leaked memo.' He might answer the question using a twenty-second soundbite that sounds like this:

'*There has been absolutely no public consultation about building a motorway extension through our estate – or anywhere else. Indeed, the only reason we know about it at all is because of a leaked council document that surfaced last week. That is disgraceful. Our first demand is to be told exactly what is being planned and to be given the right to put our views to the planners.*'

This answer expresses the three soundbite ingredients:

- **Fact** (leaked document – secrect plans)

- **Opinion** ('That is disgraceful')

- **Solution** (rights to information and consultation)

The soundbite formula is a general guideline that does not have to be complied with every time; indeed, it will be difficult to do so if you are participating in a heated interview or debate when a number of questions or comments are being thrown around. But it provides a useful basis for planning your responses for a straightforward interview.

You don't know?

If you do not know the answer to a question never say so. The reason you don't know is probably because a question that you failed to anticipate has been sprung on you. Simply say something along the lines of: 'Well, I don't have all the information in front of me, but what I do think is important is . . .' Politicians get away with it every day.

Avoidance

Exactly the same technique can be used to avoid answering questions altogether, and, again, it happens all the time. Supposing it is rumoured that Easthampton City Council is going to make mass redundancies among its manual workforce. The unions launch a vigorous campaign, and the Chief Executive of the council is interviewed on Radio LCR. The appropriate question would be:

'*Is it true that your council is planning to make sweeping redundancies among the manual workforce?*'

To which the Chief Executive might reply:

'*My council has a duty to provide a cost-effective and efficient service for the people of Easthampton and Rossbury. We constantly review all aspects of our work and will continue to do so.*'

Remember that few radio interviewers are persistent; most just want to get the interview completed and ready for broadcast. If you refuse to budge on a question then there is little that the interviewer can do about it.

Out of a corner

The more skilful interviewee will learn how to have an argument in mind that will counter any pressure that an interviewer might try to impose. On the question of redundancies the persistent interviewer might respond:

'*But have any recent reviews identified savings that can be made by imposing redundancies among the staff at Easthampton City Council?*'

This is a tricky question to avoid because it has been avoided once already, and the question has been restated in a more pointed and specific way. The response could be:

'*Easthampton City Council is a democratic organization. I cannot sit here and dictate policy – those types of decision are for the council as a whole to make. No doubt the appropriate committee will make an appropriate decision at the appropriate time.*'

A good soundbite, and one that really blocks the question from being asked again because the Chief Executive has absolutely no idea of what the council might be doing next week or next month. So the interview would have to move on to the next question or come to an end at that point.

Try again

For any type of pre-recorded interview – whether studio, location or telephone – it is possible to stop the interview at any time and start again if you make a mistake or give a totally incoherent answer. Simply stop; tell the interviewer that you would like to take that question again; and ask her to repeat the question. Then have a second bite at the cherry. But, once again, beware. During the 1992 General Election Campaign a leading politician stopped dead in the middle of an answer and asked if he could take it again. The interviewer responded that as the programme was going out live he might as well move on to the next question!

Headphones

You will be required to wear headphones in two types of interview: down-the-line interviews, and with phone-ins. Using headphones presents one major difficulty for the interviewee – you cannot hear your own voice properly. As far as you are concerned your voice sounds very muffled and wooden. This can cause your performance to suffer as you might start to speak very loudly or keep the pitch of your voice on one note, rather like a Dalek. The trick for using headphones is to keep one headphone over one ear, and slide the other one off the other ear. That way you can hear through the headphones and hear your own voice simultaneously.

Phone-ins

There are one or two points to bear in mind about phone-ins. The first one is that if you are asked to participate in a phone-in it will be because you are an acknowledged expert in a particular subject. But always be on your guard. If your area of expertise is one where the recipient of your advice could in some way be harmed by taking advice that may not be appropriate, it is always useful to add a caveat to whatever advice you do give. For example: '. . . but *do* go and see your doctor as well just to be sure.' Or, '. . . if that doesn't work then you are really advised to see a solicitor for legal advice.'

The only other practical advice about phone-ins is to take a small notebook and pencil with you so that you can make a brief note of the callers' names and points. This helps if you discuss any of the earlier calls later on in the programme.

CALLING PHONE-IN PROGRAMMES

It has been said that radio phone-in programmes are the lowest form of radio. This may or may not be the case, but one thing is certain – phone-ins are incredibly popular and command very large audiences. Therefore they provide an ideal opportunity for individuals and organizations to broadcast to – and influence – a large number of people. There are basically two types of radio phone-in: the open-line phone-in which invites calls on almost any subject; and the specialist phone-in where a guest expert, such as a solicitor or gardener, provides expert advice on his or her specialist subject. Some radio stations, such as London's LBC station, have phone-ins on an almost continuous basis. Others, including local stations operated by both the BBC and the independent network, will incorporate the phone-in into prime-time programmes, which are broadcast 10.00–12.00 a.m., 2.00–5.00 p.m. and in the early evening.

There are a number of points to remember when planning to take part in a phone-in:

- **Preparation:** the presenter and specialist are likely to be very experienced broadcasters. Therefore, to make an impact you should be well prepared with your presentation. As with radio interviews you should prepare a brief note of no more than three or four points that you want to get across in the phone-in. Remember that phone-ins are primarily concerned with opinions rather than hard facts, but you will need to back up your opinions with evidence. Keep the detail of these points to an absolute minimum as they are intended as a memory jogger – not a script. You should also prepare a brief one-sentence summary of what you want to say on the programme. We will see why that is needed in 'phoning-in', below.

- **Timing:** it is quite possible that a phone-in will go on for up to an hour if not longer, so you will need to consider the timing of your contribution. If you are calling a general open-line phone-in then you may want to call the station in the ten minute lead-up to the beginning of the broadcast to ensure that you are well ahead in the queue. But there are other timing considerations, particularly if you are calling a phone-in that is dealing with a specific subject. For example, the early callers to a phone-in effectively set the agenda for the programme; but by telephoning during the middle part of a programme, you can attempt to counter some of the earlier arguments and steer the programme in a particular direction. However, if your contribution can fit into the end part of the programme you may have the last say in the debate or, at least, your point of view will be more memorable that many of the earlier contributions. It is for you to become familiar with the format of particular phone-ins and assess the timing of your contribution in order to have the maximum impact.

- **Phoning-in:** in order to make a contribution to a radio phone-in you will obviously need access to both a radio and a telephone. You will also need to know the station's phone-in number (this is often repeatedly given out on the airwaves); have at hand your list of the three or four main points you plan to make; and also your one-line summary. The purpose of the one-line summary is that as soon as your call is answered by the radio station, the person answering – usually a producer or researcher – will ask you what the point is that you wish to make. This is done to assess whether your contribution fits the format of the programme and, possibly, to judge whether you are a suitable contributor to the programme. As soon as you get through to the station you should turn off your radio, otherwise it causes all sorts of technical problems including a form of electronic feedback called 'howling'. The producer may tell you whether or not your contribution will be used, or she will take your telephone number and say that she may call you back during the programme. In that case you will need to continue listening to the phone-in and keep an ear open for the telephone.

• **On air**: once the station has confirmed that your contribution will be used, you will have to hang on while you wait for the programme presenter to come to your call. During the waiting period you will be able to hear the programme over the telephone, so you will keep up to date on the debate and be able to monitor any further contributions. The presenter will then simply announce that you are the next caller ('Well, we now go over to David from Muswell Hill. Hi, David, what point would you like to make . . .?'). You are now on the air. Take it easy – don't rush the points you want to make. Try to think of the phone-in as a private conversation between yourself and one or two other people. Take a brief pause between sentences so that the programme host can intervene to ask salient questions or to allow the expert to make a contribution. The phone-in is the easiest type of broadcast to handle and, for the more nervous novice, good experience before tackling other types of broadcast interviews.

How to get publicity for free – radio interview checklist

• Be prepared. Write a short checklist of four or five prompt points for the interview, and take a copy of your press release with you. Take a small bottle of still mineral water with you to the studio.

- Arrive in plenty of time so that you are relaxed and well prepared for the interview.
- Do not take mobile telephones, bleeps or digital watches into the studio as these can cause embarrassing problems.
- Answer in soundbites of twenty to thirty seconds in length made up of: problem; opinion; solution.
- To allay any nerves try to think of the interview as a cosy chat between yourself, the interviewer and one listener.

6

The television interview

Although this country is served by thousands of newspapers and hundreds of radio stations, it is served by only four terrestrial television channels and only one satellite channel that broadcasts news and current affairs programmes. Many of the regional Channel 3 stations broadcast only half an hour of news and current affairs of their own each day; therefore competition between stories for the news slots is very strong indeed. However, when planning your publicity campaign bear in mind the following points:

- Although the availability of time is relatively small, the programme makers know that to be the case. Accordingly they home in on strong, community-based news stories, and prefer items that also have a good human interest content and that are highly visual.

- Television is an extremely expensive process by comparison with newspapers and radio, and so resources are very stretched. It may be that they are unable to cover your event despite its importance to you or your community.

- Because of the expense and the minimal resources available to the producers of regional television news programmes, the maxim of 'do as much of their job

for them as possible' is fitting yet again. Well
prepared and presented press releases and
backgrounders will certainly be well received even if
the event or issue fails to achieve coverage.

There are three types of television interview that will concern
the publicist at a local level:

Location

This is the most common type of interview because for many
community-based news stories it is appropriate, and sometimes even necessary, for the interview to be conducted on
location. Consider both the Veronica Green publicity event at
Easthampton General Hospital and Gary Bysouth's campaign
on the Whiteoak estate (see Chapter 2). Veronica's story
would only make any sense on television if there were location
shots of the sculpture being presented to the children's ward.
Although Gary's story could be covered without any location
shots or interviews – just as straightforward narrative from
the newscaster – it is precisely the type of topical and human-
interest story that invites location shots and location
interviews. And that is probably what would happen if Gary
sent his press release to the regional television news desks.
Like their counterparts in the radio industry, television
producers also like having interviews on tape that can be
edited into a particular slot.

Studio

As producers prefer recorded interviews on tape, and as the
main news programme is only thirty minutes in length, very
few people are invited to be interviewed live in the studio.
Those who are are usually involved in issues or events that are
major news stories in the region. Again, like their radio
counterparts, television producers would rather not have
unknown quantities (and qualities) being interviewed for live
broadcast.

Down the line

Television stations conduct interviews 'down the line' much
like the radio stations if the interviewee happens to be in the
wrong part of the country. 'Down-the-liners' on television are
usually conducted by one of the London-based national
channels, which links up with a studio elsewhere in the
country. Often the type of person interviewed is a politician or
academic. But a local story that attracts national attention
may require the local participants to be interviewed down the
line from their neck of the woods. The interviewee may be
summoned to a regional television studio, although due to the
advance of technology many BBC radio stations now have
down-the-line television facilities that link up with Television
Centre in London.

Many people are petrified of the idea of appearing on
television – others would jump at any opportunity of being
interviewed for the small screen. As a publicist it is entirely up
to you to decide whether or not to involve the regional
television stations in your particular case. You are under no
obligation to send them your press release or give an
interview. But why be so modest? Consider some of our most
popular and colourful television personalities, such as Patrick
Moore, the late Dr Magnus Pyke or Dr David Bellamy. Their
eccentricity adds to their charm. If they can get away with it
then so can you. So why not send the local TV station your
press release?

Preparation

Dress

What you wear for your television interview will clearly have
a major impact on the viewers. With television interviews it is
essential to dress smartly but plainly. Formal attire such as
suits are not always necessary, but dress for the part. If you
are wearing casual dress then at least wear your best casual
clothes. Always avoid large or loud patterns, and avoid checks
as these tend to distort when televized, which may distract

your audience. Go for plain designs and soft, pastel colours. As you will be wanting to win support for your cause or point of view then it is up to you to do everything possible to impress your audience.

Presentation

Apart from your dress there will be a few other preliminary tasks that you may wish to do before your interview is broadcast. Although you will be professionally made up on arrival at the studio, you may wish to wash and style your hair and shave – if you have enough time – before leaving for the studio. It is advisable to agree to be made up, whatever your sex, as this will improve your image and allow you to blend in with the presenters who will also be made up. It is also advisable, particularly for men, to remove the make-up before leaving the studio building. One word of warning to anyone who wears the type of glasses that automatically darken as the light increases: do not wear them for the interview as they may make you look like a representative of the Mafia.

Don't forget

Take with you to the studio your prompt points, a copy of the press release and any backgrounders that you may have sent out. You will probably have a brief discussion about the interview with the producer before the transmission, and it will be useful to have this material with you. Apart from the prompt points, this material will not actually be needed in the studio.

Getting there

Ensure that you have double checked the time of the interview and the time that you are expected at the studio. The timing will be more precise than with a radio interview because not only will you need to be made up before the programme, but the producer may also need to discuss the subject of the interview with you before the interview goes ahead. If the producer has arranged for a car to collect you then be certain of the time and location of the pick-up. If you are driving to the studio then ensure that you have an appropriate street map with you. It is worth planning your route in advance.

Get it taped!

It is very unlikely that the television station will be able to provide you with a video recording of the programme, and so you may wish to make arrangements for it to be recorded for you during the transmission.

The interview

Nerves

Not only will your audience hear you, but they will of course be able to see you on television. Therefore any sign of nerves will clearly be more apparent. The hints given on pages 75–76 for radio interviews can also be applied to television interviews. The main difference is that the television studio will provide you with refreshments both prior to and during the interview. Some television stations – particularly national channels – may invite the interviewee to the 'hospitality suite', which has a well-stocked drinks cabinet. Not only are guests able to choose from a range of alcoholic drinks, but they may be offered very sizeable measures. Simply decline the offer. Never rely on alcohol to relax you prior to a television interview as it does far more harm than good: it will cause slight dehydration resulting in an increased chance of 'dry mouth'; it may even cause your speech to slur slightly, although you may not notice the effect yourself; and, most important of all, it slows down the speed at which you respond to questions and articulate your case.

The studio

Once you have been made up and have had a brief chat with the producer about the angle of the interview, you will be taken into the studio by a member of the production team who will introduce you to the interviewer and show you to your seat. You should make sure that a drink of water is available to you in the studio. This will all happen before the programme starts, during a commercial break or whilst a pre-recorded news item is being broadcast. You may have several minutes to wait before your interview takes place. This can be put to good use, and if you are nervous it might help to undertake the following routine:

Try the breathing exercise described on page 76; make yourself comfortable; clear your throat; take a sip of water; just sit back and try to unclutter your mind. The chances are that the chair you are sitting in is a swivel chair, and it is extremely easy to swivel yourself without even noticing. Therefore, face the seat in the direction of the interviewer, and sit comfortably with both feet firmly on the ground. If, out of nerves, you *must* agitate a part of your body then try wriggling your toes inside your shoes, or play with a pen under the table. Just relax, and try to conduct the interview like any other one-to-one conversation.

Prompt points

Although the list of prompt points is a useful aid in radio interviews, it should be avoided if at all possible for television interviews. This is because the viewers will see that you are reading from prepared material and this destroys the spontaneity of the interview. However, in case of an emergency – such as your mind going completely blank – the prompt points might be useful. They can be taken into the interview and left discreetly on the table in front of you.

The interview begins

When being interviewed in a television studio do try to ignore everything in the studio except the interviewer. A television studio may strike you as being a fascinating place full of interesting pieces of photographic and sound-recording equipment. Just ignore it all. Do not look at the cameras during the interview. Establish and maintain eye contact with the interviewer. In terms of body language there are two key tips to remember if at all possible. Firstly, during the interview try to lean forward a little as this signifies attentiveness and goes down well in the viewer's mind. Secondly, tilt your head very slightly towards the interviewer. This shows that you are paying close attention to the question. In the days before the broadcast, study interviews on television news programmes to gauge just how subtle but effective body language can be. Try also to keep your hands in your lap throughout the interview, as hand gestures are very distracting on screen.

Otherwise the interview will follow the structure of a radio interview: answer in soundbites; have four or five key points in mind that you need to get across during the interview; keep cool, calm and collected. Think of the interviewer as a friend, and respond as though the interview is little more than a conversation being watched by one other person. The interview will be over a lot sooner than you think, and once it has finished sit still and say nothing, as the studio will probably still be 'on air' and you should assume that anything else you might say will be broadcast. Sit still and quietly – only get up once you are invited to.

After the interview
Relax. There is no turning the clock back. Either feel good about the interview or reflect upon your performance and consider ways that it can be improved in future. You may again be invited to take advantage of the hospitality suite, and this time you may wish to accept. As with any contact with the press and broacast media, do make a note of the producer's name (not the interviewer's name) for future reference as you can add him or her to your mailing list.

Tips for location interviews and 'down-the-liners'
Location interviews are quicker, simpler and more spontaneous than any studio interview. The interview will probably be edited down to a minute or minute-and-a-half, and will normally consist of a close-up shot of your head and shoulders. You should ignore the camera; maintain eye

contact with the interviewer; and try to give your answers in soundbites. Try to stand perfectly still and avoid gesticulating with your hands. Plan ahead, if possible, by bringing a brush or comb and a mirror with you to the event being covered by the television station.

With a 'down-the-liner' you will be sitting in front of a microphone and a fixed-position, unstaffed camera. There may also be one or two monitors – television sets – positioned for you to see. These will show the scenes in the recipient studio, and show you sitting in front of the camera in front of you. Instead of headphones, there will be an ear-piece through which you will hear the producer and interviewer talking to you. Completely ignore the pictures on the monitors. Think of the centre of the lens on the camera as the interviewer's eye, and keep eye contact with the camera throughout the interview. Do not let your gaze drift to the monitors to see what is going on in the recipient studio. Most viewers appreciate that 'down the line' interviews are difficult to participate in simply because you are not in the same room as the person talking to you. Hence your audience will sympathize with you if you experience any problems.

How to get publicity for free – television interview checklist

- Most television interviews will be very short. Make sure that you have four or five key points that you want to get across.
- Your preparation should include: hair; shave; smart but sober dress; travel arrangements; prompt points; press release and backgrounders.
- When in the studio waiting for the interview to start sit still and straight; keep your hands and feet motionless if possible; position yourself towards the interviewer.
- During the interview maintain eye contact at all times; lean slightly towards the interviewer,

remembering not to swivel on the chair or gesticulate with your hands.

- After the interview make a note of the producer's name and ensure that she or he receives future press releases and backgrounders.

7

Photographs

The old saying tells us that 'a picture is worth a thousand words'. In publicity terms this means that any event should be geared up to be as visual as possible and therefore attract the interest of the picture editors of the local press – and perhaps the national newspapers. Even the briefest glance at the news pages of national and local newspapers will reveal that often the photograph often more than doubles the amount of editorial space given over to a news item. Indeed, in some cases the picture itself makes the story where there may otherwise have been no story. It is even possible to create news by thinking up exciting and original visual ideas – known in journalism as the photo-opportunity – and literally manufacture news.

A little imagination can produce a very simple photo-opportunity that can have a major impact with the media. Civil rights campaigners discovered this when they attended a meeting at the House of Commons on official secrecy and freedom of speech. Before the meeting the participants simply stood in a group outside the Houses of Parliament gagged by handkerchiefs tied around their mouths. This simple photo-opportunity generated widespread publicity on television news programmes and in the press.

The type of events that make good photo-opportunities include:

- **Picket:** this is perhaps one of the most common

photo-opportunities to appear in newspapers – a group of people standing outside a building, or other location, with a number of placards bearing simple slogans. Although this is a well tried and tested photo-opportunity, pickets clearly contain the three essential news-making ingredients: human interest; topicality; and conflict. Keep the slogans on the placards as clear and simple as possible, and try to add some originality to the event (see the section on leaflets, below).

- **Petition:** the handing-in of a petition to a politician or other official will be as familiar to the public as a picket; indeed, the two events can often be combined. However, collecting signatures for a petition can be time-consuming compared with staging a picket, which can often be quickly organized and brought into action.

- **Leafleting:** the sight of a group of activists handing out leaflets in the High Street on a Saturday morning will generate little enthusiasm in a newspaper's picture editor. However, the sight of a group of activists dressed in bizarre fancy dress might prompt the newspaper to cover the event. Members of Friends of the Earth dressed in khaki shorts and deer-stalkers, or anti-pollution campaigners wearing gas masks, could well result in the local newspaper sending a photographer along to capture an otherwise routine campaign event.

- **Funerals:** although few British prime ministers have died in office, dozens of funeral processions have passed up and down Downing Street as campaigners and activists have demonstrated against the death, or threatened death, of communities, industries, hospitals, jobs, schools, neighbourhoods and all manner of community resources. The mock funeral is a very potent campaign tool and photo-opportunity, and is unlikely to go unnoticed by the media at a local level. A dummy coffin is an easy prop to produce; top hats and tails all round will make the event even more eye-catching and more successful as a campaign event.

- **Children:** if appropriate, do try to include children in the photo-opportunity as they can have a major impact on the coverage. Children add significantly to the human interest aspect of the event – particularly for the popular end of the press. Children are just as affected by the world around them as adults are, so they can be equally involved in campaign issues and events. As Veronica Green will have found out with her press release about the presentation at her local hospital, children almost guarantee the success of a photo-opportunity, particularly when they share the pain and problems of the adult world.

- **Evidence:** take evidence of your case with you to the photo-opportunity. For example, Greenpeace protesters once (illegally) dumped radioactive earth outside the Westminster offices of the Department of the Environment in a protest against nuclear power generation. On a slightly lesser scale your campaign may also have evidence in its possession that can be presented to the media at a photo-opportunity. For example, low-paid workers could display their pay slips to the camera; or a householder subject to a compulsory purchase order could present the official documents at the photo-opportunity for all the world to see.

- **Stunts:** although much more risky than straightforward photo-opportunities, publicity stunts can generate substantial coverage of an event. Abseilers from Greenpeace found this to be the case when they scaled Big Ben and draped a huge banner down the world-famous tourist attraction. Although the protesters were eventually arrested, they had caused no actual damage and they were let off with a police caution.

Similarly, gay rights activists worried about the spread of Aids in Britain's prisons developed a remarkably simple technique for reducing the Aids problem and generating publicity at a stroke – they simply catapulted packets of condoms over prison walls around the country. This was a straightforward publicity stunt that gained widespread attention at an international level. However, before staging any type of publicity stunt do thoroughly consider all angles of the plan – particularly the safety and legal implications which need to be given priority at the planning stage and throughout the stunt.

Picture press releases

When planning a photo-opportunity it is worthwhile producing an additional press release for the newspaper's picture editor. It needs to be shorter than a normal press release as it is unnecessary to include any quotes. Just give the who, what, where and when details; there is no need to tell the picture editor *why* the event is taking place as she will be able to assess the event's news value at a glance. Veronica Green's press release on the Easthampton General Hospital publicity event can be easily adapted for the picture editor:

GREEN'S THE FLORIST

27 High Street
Rossbury
Nr Easthampton
Leighshire, EH4 2FL
Tel: Easthampton 654321

PRESS RELEASE: FOR IMMEDIATE RELEASE   14th April 1993

MAYOR HANDS OVER CASTLE TO SICK CHILDREN

The Mayor of Easthampton, Councillor Lizzy White, will next week present a massive floral sculpture of Rossbury Castle to patients in the children's ward at Easthampton General Hospital. The 1.5-metre-high floral sculpture will be collected from Green's by the Mayoral limousine at 2.30pm on Wednesday 21st April 1993 and transported to Easthampton General Hospital for a 3.00pm presentation.

ENDS

FOR FURTHER INFORMATION: Veronica Green, Easthampton 654321

The additional cost of about 50p will be a worthwhile investment to ensure that the picture editor is briefed about the event well in advance of the photo-opportunity. Remember, the picture alone can more than double the amount of editorial space allocated to your news story.

Picture ideas letter

Picture editors are often keen to hear about unusual events that will make interesting photo-features. It is possible for anyone to send an ideas letter to the picture editor suggesting that the event is covered. Here is an example of an ideas letter sent to the picture editor of the *Independent* newspaper by a freelance journalist:

Dear Chris McKane
   BEATING THE BOUNDS – THURSDAY 4TH MAY,
2.30PM
   *Few maps existed during the Middle Ages, so an annual
ritual of Beating the Bounds developed to commemorate
parish boundaries throughout England. In London, this event
still takes place each year when a Port of London Authority
launch takes a procession of Masters of the Livery
Companies, and other dignitaries, out to a marker in the
middle of the River Thames. Once there a schoolboy from St
Dunstans College, Catford, is held upside-down by the ankles
over the side of the boat while he whacks the boundary.*
   A perfect photo-opportunity for the Independent. *I have
conducted some research into this unusual event and plan to
be to be there on the 4th. If you would like to send a
photographer along to accompany me then do give me a call.*
   Yours sincerely . . .

This letter certainly did the trick as the Beating the Bounds
Ceremony was duly covered by the *Independent*, which
published a prominent photo-feature in its 5th May edition.
All that is needed is a straightforward ideas letter, and
possibly a follow-up phone call.

Mugshots

The final photographic aid to the publicist is the mugshot. A
mugshot is a small head and shoulders photograph, of the
type that frequently appears in news and feature articles. A
local newspaper, for example, will have a mugshot library of
all councillors, the local Member of Parliament and any other
prominent local figures who routinely appear in the news.
   The newspaper may want to include your mugshot in its
library if it is likely that you are going to make repeat appear-
ances in the newspaper's news pages. The picture editor may
arrange for a staff photographer to take the mugshot. Otherwise
you can always submit a simple portrait photograph to the

newspaper with your original press release – once again saving the newspaper a job. However, this may involve some expense unless you know a competent amateur photographer who is prepared to help. The photograph should be a straightforward head-on pose of your head and shoulders. The photograph should be black and white and printed on glossy paper to the approximate size of 153 mm x 103 mm (6 in x 4 in), which will be reduced to its working size in the newspaper printing process.

How to get publicity for free – photographs

- Make it visual! When planning your publicity campaign create highly visual events that will attract the attention of the picture editor.
- Plan unusual angles to your campaign such as fancy dress, eye-catching props or examples of evidence. Remember that children will considerably amplify the human interest quality of many campaign activities and photo-opportunities.
- Press release the photo-opportunity. Invest another 50p in sending a short press release to the newspaper's picture editor – it could double the coverage of your event.
- Send a picture ideas letter to the picture editor outlining any additional aspects of your campaign that are interesting or unusual.

8

Press conferences

A press conference – also known as a news conference – is a meeting organized by the person or organization that is making the news, where journalists from newspapers, radio stations and television news programmes are invited to hear what the publicist has to say and to ask questions. We have all seen press conferences on the television news: two or three smart individuals sitting behind a table surrounded by microphones, photographers, journalists, lights and television cameras.

The press conference can be an extremely powerful publicity tool, as you control the whole event, including the precise timing of your news becoming public. But the general rule about press conferences is – don't. Most news stories are adequately communicated by publishing a press release and backgrounders. Press conferences are only ever staged when there is something *very* important to announce, or when there is something to announce that can not possibly be covered by a press release.

The type of events that may be fitting for a press conference include:

- The launch of a major new campaign or initiative, such as the setting up of a local branch of an environmental pressure group or a campaign to protest against a controversial council planning decision.

- The presence of an important visitor; this could possibly be a household name, such as a politician or famous broadcaster, who has agreed to speak at a public meeting.

- The publication of an important new book, report or other document. For example, the local environmental campaign group might publish a report on local factories that fail to comply with the law on pollution.

- A demonstration: show it to the world. For example, if your St John's Ambulance group has just taken delivery of the latest type of ambulance, don't talk about it – demonstrate it!

- To dispel a major rumour or controversy – to put the record straight.

But beware. If you decide to organize a press conference about a subject that could have been adequately publicized by using a press release and backgrounder, then journalists may be very wary of attending future events staged by your organization. This can do you untold damage and, although it is possible to obtain publicity for free, it does actually have a price – trust. Journalists certainly have to trust you to give them accurate on-the-record information, and in return you receive free publicity in print and on the air. While you can increase the chances of obtaining free publicity by doing the bulk of the journalists' work for them, it equally applies that by wasting a journalist's time you are considerably reducing your chances of media coverage.

Types of press conference

In effect there are three types of press conference:

Formal press conference

This is an event that is nothing but a well-planned press conference that is set up solely for the purpose of briefing the media.

Spontaneous press conference

Certain types of event automatically attract the attention of the media, and press conferences can sometimes take place at very short notice. One example could be when a famous or controversial figure is acquitted at the Old Bailey or the High Court, and the subject and the lawyers concerned issue statements and answer questions from journalists outside the court. Spontaneous press conferences also take place at the scenes of major crimes or disasters.

Public meetings

Sometimes the only difference between a public meeting and a formal press conference is the presence of the public. It is possible to gear up a public meeting to have all the benefits of a press conference.

Timing

The timing of your press conference will be a major factor not only in the planning of the conference itself, but also in your overall media campaign. For example, if Gary Bysouth finds out that Easthampton City Council is going to consider the motorway extension at the council's meeting on the following Wednesday evening, then it might be appropriate to stage a press conference on the Wednesday morning – if the campaign has something new to tell the world. Indeed, this might be the ideal opportunity to launch the campaign formally. The news would hit the Wednesday lunchtime radio and television news bulletins, and also the local evening newspaper and the main early evening television news magazine programme. Therefore, the issues and views of Gary's campaign will be dominating the news during the media's coverage of the council meeting –

as the news would be going out shortly before the council's meeting takes place – and this may well allow the campaign to exert considerable influence on the debate in the council chamber. *You* control the timing of the press conference, and therefore *you* can manipulate the timing to your advantage.

Here are some other factors in the timing of a press conference:

Avoid strong news days

Try to avoid staging a press conference that clashes with any major events that are taking place in your locality – major sporting events or festivals, for example. Such a clash will mean that your event will compete for press attention and for newspaper space and air time. Other times when major national news events are taking place, such as elections or the State opening of Parliament, should also be avoided if possible.

Choose clear news days

If the timing of your event is flexible – that is to say it does not tie in with any other event such as a council meeting and you can pick and choose the day of the press conference – then you may want to select a weak news day. Traditionally these are Monday and Friday, and news events breaking on those days may receive greater news coverage than on other days. But it will be for you to judge the importance of your press conference and whether it will compete strongly with other news events. It is an art, and one way of assessing the relative news value of events is to study the local press – and radio and television news programmes – to observe what type of events gain prominent news coverage.

Deadlines

The time of day is also an important factor in the planning of a press conference. Generally speaking, a press conference should be in the late morning – around 10.30 or 11.00 a.m. This is because the evening newspaper will have a deadline of around 2.00 p.m. for its first edition. This will coincide with the lunchtime radio and television news bulletins, and local items that appear on lunchtime bulletins are often repeated on early evening programmes. Later bulletins may even run an extended version of the earlier story.

Time of year

If you are launching a campaign or perhaps a new product, and are completely flexible about the timing of your press conference, then it may be beneficial to consider times of the year when publicity can more easily be obtained. The summer holiday period is known as the 'silly season', and this particularly applies to the month of August. This is because Parliament is in recess, and many other organizations are taking a summer break and therefore not generating news. These include local government authorities, academic institutions and many voluntary sector organizations. In the summer news is scarce, and seemingly trivial issues begin to fill the newspapers and airwaves. This, of course, gives the publicist the opportunity to take advantage of the lack of news. But it has one obvious drawback – if it is the holiday season and many people are away, then your potentially high-profile media campaign will be missed by some of your target audience.

But there are strategically useful parts of the silly season that are ideal for planning media events. The key time is mid- to late September. Once the autumn school term starts many holidaymakers are back at home and will start reading the newspapers, watching television and listening to the radio. Parliament will still be in recess – until the middle of October at least – and many other news-making organizations such as councils and government agencies will still be operating at a reduced level. Therefore your audience is in place, and yet the media is still short of news. You could take advantage of that situation.

Press release

The announcement of a press conference is made by using the standard press release. However, there will be a few changes:

Why?

Although the press release sent out to announce your press conference will state the who, what, where and when it is happening, it must go to great lengths to stress the *why*. Why is this subject so important that it warrants a press conference? Spell it out very clearly and convince the journalist that she cannot avoid attending your event.

Embargo

A press conference is just the type of event that requires an embargo to be attached to the press release, as this will ensure that there will be no publicity until after the press conference. This will give you the opportunity to speak candidly with journalists prior to the press conference, knowing that nothing will be published or broadcast until the embargo date and time. It is usually appropriate to put the time of the press conference as the embargo.

Venue

The venue for a press conference should be as central and accessible to the media as possible. A local community centre or church hall may be suitable; commercial organizations may book a conference room at a hotel in which to stage their press conference – a particularly costly option. Whatever the nature of your chosen venue, it should, ideally, have the following facilities.

Parking

There should either be a parking lot attached to the venue, or adequate street parking available nearby. This will obviously be necessary for radio cars or outside broadcast units attending the conference. Others attending the conference, including newspaper journalists and your own supporters, will want to avoid a lengthy walk to the venue.

Seating

The size of the room used for the conference should adequately house all those who might attend, but avoid an oversized room or hall as it may give the impression that the event is poorly attended. For a successful local press conference you can expect two television crews of about three people each; one or two radio journalists; and as many newspaper journalists as there are newspapers in your area – plus the same number of press photographers. This will give a total of roughly twelve media people at your press conference if it is being staged in a large town or city, and of course there will probably be other members of your campaign or company present. So you may need a room that can adequately seat twenty or twenty-five people. Also take into account that the television cameras and lights will take up some space towards the back of the venue.

Power points

The television crews will need access to ordinary mains electricity power points in which to plug their lights. Ensure that an adequate electricity supply is available. Also ensure that there is adequate overhead lighting near the main table which will seat the conference's hosts.

Heating

A venue that was satisfactory for a meeting in the heat of the summer might not be as satisfactory during the winter if there is no heating. Investigate the availability of heating, and also how the heating is controlled.

Refreshments

Those attending the conference will appreciate simple refreshments – tea, coffee and biscuits. Check if a kettle and crockery are available at the venue, or alternatively arrange for the necessary equipment and supplies to be brought in on the day. Ideally, arrange for someone to have responsibility for the refreshments in order to leave you free to concentrate on the press conference.

Toilets

Are there toilets at the venue? Will they be unlocked at the time of the press conference; and are they clean and adequately serviced?

Smoking

Will smoking be permitted in the press conference? If so, is there an adequate supply of ashtrays? If smoking is not permitted, are there signs prominently displayed that make it clear that smoking is prohibited?

Preparation

A successful press conference is ninety per cent organization and only ten per cent delivery. There are a number of issues that need to be planned in advance that will ensure a well-organized and professional press conference.

Booking

Although the press conference will last for little more than half an hour, the venue should be booked for at least two hours. This will allow half an hour's preparation time before the conference starts; up to forty-five minutes for the press conference itself; additional time for individual radio and television interviews immediately after the conference; and for informal interviews and discussions with journalists. The booking should also allow enough time for cleaning up after the conference.

Press packs

Although you will have already sent out press releases and backgrounders, it is useful to have press packs available at the press conference. A press pack can be made up of the press release and backgrounder(s); copies of any speeches presented at the conference; a one-sheet brief biography of the individuals hosting the conference; and a short agenda for the conference that lists its component parts and the names of the people speaking. The agenda should go at the front of the press pack, which should be presented in an A4 plastic folder. If the funds are available to produce press packs, it will be a worthwhile investment, as it gives the event a very professional touch.

Exhibition material

If your campaign or organization is long-established then it may have an exhibition display or other background material that can contribute to the presentation. For example, the Whiteoak Action Campaign may have produced a large-scale map of the Whiteoak estate and surrounding area, and marked the intended motorway route in indelible red ink. This could be mounted on a display unit or large noticeboard, perhaps together with photographic prints of scenes of the estate – a simple yet effective presentation.

Tape recorder

If possible, have a standard cassette tape recorder at the conference to record the entire event. This will be a small safeguard against any disputes over what was said at the conference, and will also give you a useful momento of the event for your organization's records. It is quite acceptable for you openly to tape-record the entire event.

Mineral water

Those presenting the press conference will probably appreciate a supply of mineral water on the top table, for much the same reasons as with a television studio interview (see Chapter 6). This can be in addition to other refreshments available at the conference.

People presentation

The press conference will in many respects be similar to the television studio interview, and so the same dress code should apply at a press conference: ensure that those appearing at the conference are dressed in plain, smart clothes that avoid loud designs. Also, take a mirror and comb or hairbrush to the conference for last-minute preparations.

The press conference

On the day of the press conference endeavour to arrive early at the venue – at least thirty minutes before it is due to begin. Make sure that the press packs, exhibition material, tape recorder, water and refreshments are also at the venue in advance. Plan enough time to set out the seats, assemble the exhibition etc. If possible, have a spare set of hands available to make the drinks, chaperone the guests, take down details of those present, and to co-ordinate requests for radio and television interviews after the conference.

The press conference itself will normally be made up of four distinct parts:

● 	The main presentation.

● 	Question-and-answer session.

● 	Interviews.

● 	Informal discussions.

The formal presentation will involve the hosts on the top table presenting their case – and any supporting evidence – to the assembled press and broadcast journalists. This will be followed by a question-and-answer session, and then the opportunity for individual interviews for the radio and television stations. Remember at all times that this is *your* press conference, and that it is up to you to keep the conference under control and on course. For example, ensure that journalists do not interrupt the main presentation but confine any questions to the later question-and-answer session.

Main presentation
The press conference will kick off with the main presentation which should last no longer than twenty of the forty-five minutes allocated to the entire press conference. Allow a margin of some five minutes for late arrivals – media folk are notorious for arriving at the very last minute. Remember that

journalists need straight-to-the-point punchy facts and quotes. Give them exactly that.

It should be clear from the start of the conference who is chairing the event. That person should call the conference to order and introduce herself or himself. The assembled journalists should be thanked for attending, and reminded that the press pack is available for their information. The other people assembled on the top table should then be introduced. If there is to be more than one speaker on the top table then make sure that each has a clear and specific task to fulfil. For example, when the Greater London Association of Community Health Councils lauched its report *Infertility Services – a Desperate Case* at a press conference, in addition to the two authors they also had two infertile couples present to give an account of their experiences. This was perfect media material, and had all the essential qualities of human interest, topicality and conflict.

Immediately following the introductions it should be made clear that a question-and-answer session will follow, and if journalists have any questions then they will be answered later. You will have some ten minutes in which to say your piece – and the local press and broadcast media are now poised on the edge of their seats ready to write their headlines. Don't let them down. Start by outlining the broad issue that your organization is confronting – then go straight into the subject that the press conference was convened to address. No doubt the members of your organization will have considered carefully why the issue was important enough to require a press conference; what campaign issues need to be presented to the press conference; and *what the campaign is now calling for to happen* – in other words, what the campaign is aiming to get out of the conference. Only you and your campaign can answer these questions, and all these points need to be thoroughly considered and thought out even before the initial press release is published. Remember, though, that the thrust of your case and any supporting evidence should be confined to about twenty minutes. If necessary, stage a dress rehearsal in front of friends to practise getting it right.

Questions and answers

Allocate ten or fifteen minutes for questions and answers. As we saw in the section on radio presentations, you do not necessarily have to provide answers that exactly match the questions, but be fair on the journalists – they are there to help you to get publicity for free, so if you believe in the subject of your campaign you should be able to provide them with the information they need to do the job.

Interviews

Although radio and television journalists may be present throughout the conference, recording all or part of your presentation, they will probably request separate interviews immediately after the formal part of the conference. This is so that each broadcast journalist can ask individual questions that relate to their particular angle on the story. Ideally, another member of your organization will be able to work out the running order of the interviews, and keep the heated hacks under some sort of control. Be prepared to repeat yourself in answering questions for each of the interviews.

Informal discussions

Once the main interviews are over you may find that there are journalists wanting to talk to you in more detail about your campaign or launch. For example, a reporter from the local newspaper may be planning to write an in-depth feature article on the subject of the press conference, or angling to act as a 'stringer' for one of the national newspapers (a stringer is a local contact for one of the national newspapers who puts forward proposals about local stories that might make the national news). Do make time for such informal discussions. Indeed, take advantage of any opportunity to build links – formal or informal – with journalists from your local newspapers, radio and television stations. But always remember that everything you say to journalists, irrespective of the setting, is on the record and liable to be reported.

The clear-up

As the key people involved in the press conference may be dealing with radio and television interviews and discussions with journalists, it will be necessary to arrange for the chaperone person, and possibly other helpers, to make sure that all items brought to the press conference – such as exhibits, refreshment equipment and the tape recorder – are removed, and that the venue is left in a tidy and respectable condition.

Once the conference has concluded you may wish to arrange for the radio and television news bulletins to be recorded, and for all the local newspapers to be checked for coverage. Check the details of all those present at the press conference against your press lists, and add the details of any newcomers to that list.

How to get publicity for free – press conference checklist

- Only stage a press conference if you have a major news story to announce, or a major new campaign, publication or product to launch.
- Plan the timing of a press conference carefully: consider the strategic timing of your overall campaign around the prospect of obtaining maximum media coverage.
- When announcing the press conference ensure that your press release has a clear embargo attached to it, and that it stresses the overwhelmingly convincing reasons for the press conference taking place.
- The venue should be as central and accessible as possible, and should have adequate facilities including: parking, power points, exhibition display boards and refreshment facilities.
- Thorough preparation is essential to ensure a successful press conference. Consider carefully in

advance who is to say what, and why; plan press packs, exhibition material, refreshments and your own appearance.

- Use the conference as an opportunity to develop formal and informal contacts with journalists – but remember that you should never speak 'off the record'.

9

Letters

The letters columns of local and national newspapers are very popular and are widely read. Some letters columns – such as that in the *Guardian* – have almost cult status. Clearly a letters column has but one purpose: to give the public the opportunity of expressing their views on almost any subject. However, the letters column can also be used as part of a broad publicity campaign to supplement other forms of publicity, rather than be used in place of the press release and backgrounder.

Let's say, for example, that your campaign has received publicity in the previous week's edition of the local newspaper. Although the coverage has been fair and accurate, it was also missed out some important facts or, perhaps, unintentionally misrepresented some of the activities of your organization. The letters column is the ideal medium through which you can make corrections or additions to the news coverage, and thus increase the amount of publicity that your cause obtains. Seasoned and professional campaigners make a point of always holding back one or two salient facts or arguments so that as soon as their initial publicity starts to fade, they can provide it with some rejuvenation in the form of a letter to the letters column. Ideally, a publicity campaign will be geared up to provide the media with fresh news – in the form of regular updates on its current state of play – and can therefore obtain publicity on at least a bi-weekly basis. The letters column will be an important part of that strategy.

The letters column has the advantage of being able to accommodate contributions of a variety of lengths, ranging from one-liners, through to more lengthy, in-depth letters. Here are two examples from the *Guardian*:

Dear Sir
   To sell British Telecom is a bold step; but to sell it for cash to people who already own it is most imaginative.
Yours faithfully
M. W. REID
Abthorpe, Northamptonshire

Dear Sir
   While driving along Ashton Old Road in the general direction of Manchester city centre, my eye was caught by a large advertisement which began with the word 'Motorist'.
   Realising that the advertisement was meant to attract my attention, I averted my gaze from the road, and the cyclist riding in front of me, to the signboard. Unfortunately at this precise moment a policeman assisting a blind man with a guide dog and a man with a ladder across the road instructed the cyclist to stop.
   As my attention had been distracted by the advertisement, I ran into the cyclist causing him to be thrown forward off his bicycle and to trap his head in the rungs of the ladder.
   The force of the cyclist hitting the ladder caused the man carrying it to spin in a clockwise direction and fall over, catching the fingers of one hand in the still-spinning front wheel of the bicycle, while the ladder hit the policeman on the back of the head, knocking off his helmet and rendering him unconscious.
   The guide dog had by this time become very agitated, its harness being entangled in the bicycle pedals, and it bit the calf of the cyclist quite severely.
   As a result of being knocked to the ground by a flying saddlebag, the blind man had become disorientated and

walked into the path of a bus carrying school children. The driver however managed to avoid him, but not without mounting the pavement and knocking over a telephone kiosk trapping the occupant, a pregnant lady, and causing her to receive a series of electric shocks.

I am pleased to say that after the arrival of an ambulance, a fire engine, two police cars, the dog warden and British Telecom all was quickly back in order. But not before I had time to dwell on the words of the ad that had attracted my attention: 'Motorist, why are you looking up here, shouldn't you be watching for cyclists?' (published by the Ministry of Transport).

Yours faithfully
D. O. JONES
Audenshaw, Manchester

Make a point of studying the letters columns of the publications to which you intend to make a contribution, and learn from other people's contributions about the different styles that can be adopted when writing letters. Also, make the effort to read the letters column of a quality national newspaper occasionally, to see how the experts do it. In addition to increasing the volume of media coverage there are further advantages in using the letters column for publicity. As the column is open for everyone to use, any one contribution may generate responses that spark off a lively debate on your particular topic. In our free and democratic society such debate is sadly scarce, and newspapers provide a valuable public service in encouraging the public to have their say. But the column may also encourage your opposition – perhaps the bureaucratic officials in your community – to respond to your publicity. This can be no bad thing as it not only generates further publicity for your cause, but may also force your opponents to state their position publicly.

When writing to the letters page of a newspaper it is worth bearing in mind the following points:

Length

Newspapers vary considerably in the length of letters that they are prepared to print, although if your letter is too long it will be cut to the appropriate length. Some newspapers edit letters into the style of the particular newspaper; others will print them as written. The national broadsheet newspapers – such as the *Guardian* or the *Daily Telegraph* – may occasionally publish lengthy letters of up to 700 or 750 words on a particularly important subject. They will, of course, also publish much shorter letters and one-liners. National tabloids confine themselves to letters of no more than one or two short paragraphs. The entire letter will probably be only four or five sentences long.

The best advice is to study the letters column of the newspaper for which you intend to write, and assess the range and length of letters published. You can then tailor your contribution to fit that publication. With local newspapers it is worth bearing in mind that, from the editor's point of view, the publication of letters is a rare way of filling editorial space for free. The newspaper may even welcome the occasional lengthy contribution. You should not necessarily expect your letter to appear exactly as it was written. The editor has the ultimate right to amend or change anything that appears in her newspaper – as journalists often complain! However, if the facts or meaning of the letter suffer in the process of editing then you are in a strong position to send off another letter to correct your earlier contribution.

Layout

The layout of the letter that you send to the newspaper's letters column is basically the same as for any other type of letter: your address goes on the top right-hand side of the page, and the newspaper's address a little further down on the left. Immediately underneath the newspaper's address should be the full date, and the body of the letter starts a few lines further down. The letter should be sent to the editor impersonally, which means you do not need to know the editor's name; simply start the letter 'Dear Madam or Sir' or

'Dear Ms or Sir'. The letter should then conclude 'Yours faithfully'. The letter should be typed or word-processed on plain A4 paper – typing on one side of the paper only. Local newspapers are quite flexible about receiving handwritten letters, so long as they are very clearly written.

Bear in mind the maxim that the more work you do for the journalist – or editor – the greater are your chances of seeing your publicity in print. Therefore, ensure that your letter conforms to the length of letters published in your chosen newspaper; that it is typewritten or word-processed on to A4 paper; and remember if you type it double-spaced, then you considerably increase the chances of it being published.

Anonymity

Occasionally letters are published in newspapers that do not bear the writer's name or address. These are usually marked 'Name and address supplied', or something similar, by the editor. The only time a newspaper editor will agree to with-hold the letter-writer's identity is if the subject of the letter is highly personal or if it would be dangerous to the writer if his or her identity were to be revealed. For example, somebody writing a personal account of being a victim of some kind of crime – such as rape or other form of sexual abuse – will be granted anonymity. Otherwise editors will expect contributors to have the courage of their convictions when going public. If you require anonymity say so very clearly in a note typed immediately after your name at the end of the letter. You can always state that the letter should only be published on that basis, or not at all. In that case the editor will not use it if she is not willing to give you that anonymity.

Other requirements

Some newspapers print a short editorial statement on the letters page that sets out the requirements for their contributors – such as maximum length of letters to be submitted. This should be studied carefully and the instructions followed. For example, it may require you to give a daytime contact telephone number. This will simply be for the newspaper to verify the origin of the letter, and will not be published.

Style

The style of the letter should be as straightforward and conversational as possible. It is best to write in the first person and keep the sequence of events in a logical order. Do write from the heart if you think it will give your letter an edge, but produce at least one or two drafts before committing yourself. Read the drafts back to yourself so you can assess how they sound. If possible, produce your letter on a word processor so that you can print out draft copies and make as many changes or amendments as necessary. In order to allow your writing skills to develop there is nothing to stop you from copying the style of other people's letters; of course, the content and message of the letter will be your own.

How to get publicity for free – letters columns

- Letters columns are popular and widely read. They can be used to add to debates, correct editorial mistakes or to otherwise inform or entertain the readership.
- Write in the style and to the length that is appropriate for the intended recipient newspaper.
- Although addressed to the editor, keep the letter impersonal and, if possible, type it on to sheets of A4 paper.
- Check the letters columns of your local newspapers, and use them as a way of generating regular publicity.

10

Access programmes

Many radio and television stations broadcast access programmes that allow the public – both individuals and organizations – either to contribute directly to the making of current affairs programmes, or even to take editorial control of a particular programme or slot. Some access programmes exist simply to allow charities and voluntary organizations to publicize themselves; others allow groups to make much more detailed programmes about the services they provide or about specific campaign issues. Access programmes broadcast by the national stations and networks will require the programme's subject to have some national significance – a gripe about a small, local problem such as a road-widening scheme will not be suitable for the national access programmes, although it may fit well into an access slot on a local radio station or, possibly, the regional Channel 3 television station. Access programmes will vary considerably from area to area, and may only be broadcast for part of the year.

If you decide to apply to a radio or television station to make an access programme then you should find out from the very outset what, exactly, is required from you. Some programmes will merely require you to send in material to the station. Others, such as the major access television programmes, may involve you full time for many weeks or even months. How many hours of work will it involve? Will any travelling be required? Will you be expected to undertake any of the scripting, or to appear on-screen? Be prepared.

Letters and 'right to reply' programmes

These are popular slots that allow individual members of the public to comment on programmes broadcast on the national radio and television networks. The most popular are *Points of View* on BBC television; and *Right to Reply* on Channel 4. *Points of View* allows the public to write in complaint – or praise – to the BBC about any aspect of its output; and *Right to Reply* fulfils a similar role for the independent television network.

Right to Reply has two features in addition to the reading-out of letters. The Channel 4 programme does invite members of the public to engage in face-to-face debates with pro-gramme makers; and it also operates a series of Video Boxes throughout the country. These allow members of the public to sit inside a small booth, rather like a passport photograph booth, and record a short videotaped contribution for the programme.

The programme addresses are:

Points of View
BBC Television Centre
Wood Lane
London W12 8QT
Tel: 071-7643 8000

Right to Reply
Channel 4
60 Charlotte Street
London W1P 2AX
Tel: 071-631 4000

Community access slots

These are short and simple access slots of between thirty seconds and one minute that are often made available by the regional independent television stations and some local radio stations. They are rather like simple commercials, giving out basic details about the work of a group or organization. However, they are often limited to charities or charitable appeals. To find out exactly what is currently available in your region, you should check the television and radio listings magazines. Alternatively you can telephone the duty officer of the television or radio stations that serve your area.

Access programmes

These are programmes where voluntary groups or campaigning organizations are able to make entire programmes and retain editorial control of what they make. The most well known of these programmes is the BBC's *Open Space* programme which offers a regular thirty-minute slot on BBC2. Channel 4 also offers an access programme in the form of *Free For All*. To participate in programmes of this nature can be very demanding: for successful applicants the making of the programme can involve many weeks of very hard work.

However, that hard work can pay off. In 1990 a pressure group, the Campaign Against Arms Trade (CAAT), made a thirty-minute programme for *Open Space* on the arms trade in the post-glasnost era. In the week following the programme's transmission CAAT received more than 1000 membership enquiries from the public. So be prepared for the consequences of obtaining free publicity. Both *Open Space* and *Free for All* publish explanatory guidance notes for potential applicants. They can be contacted at the following addresses:

Open Space
Community Programme Unit
BBC TV
Room 10
39 Wales Farm Road
London W3 6UP
Tel: 071-743 8000 ext 3511

Free for All
Filmit Productions Limited
2 Tunstall Road
London SW9 8BN
Tel: 071-738 4175
Fax: 071-738 3787

There are additional, relatively minor, access slots available on national radio and television. BBC Radio 4 broadcasts a series called *Punters* which allows individuals to raise issues of personal interest; Channel 4 broadcasts *Comment* after each evening edition of the Channel 4 News; and the Radio 4 *PM* programme has a regular letters slot. *Punters* can be contacted at:

BBC South & West
Broadcasting House
Whiteladies Road
Bristol
Avon BS8 2LR
Tel: (0272) 732211

Proposals for the Channel 4 *Comment* slot can be sent to:

Comment
Channel 4
60 Charlotte Street
London W1P 2AX
Tel: 071-631 4000

Specialist programmes
Various groups have succeeded in obtaining space on the airwaves in order to tackle issues that are specific to their communities. For example, lesbians and gay men have a regular series called *Out* on Channel 4; Jews have a weekly programme on London's LBC radio station entitled *You Don't Have To Be Jewish*; the London Irish community has a regular half-hour programme on the BBC's GLR radio

station; and that well-known majority, women, are still thoughtfully provided with their regular slot, *Woman's Hour*, on BBC Radio 4. The disabled, Afro-Caribbeans and the Asian community are also specific groups that have specialist programmes on both radio and television. Such programmes often rely upon outside contributions, and can often be used to obtain access to the airwaves.

Investigative programmes

In addition to the national press, the major television and radio stations broadcast investigative programmes that can include cases or items that originate as local stories and campaigns. Although such programmes can be contacted directly it is worth noting that the issues they take up are invariably of national significance, and if they do pursue an issue that originates at a local level then it is usually because it first receives initial coverage in the local and regional media. However, if your subject has a strong investigative angle then it may be useful to contact one or more of the following. For example, Esther Rantzen's *That's Life* programme has an infamous reputation for penetrative investigative journalism on a range of social policy issues.

Face The Facts
BBC Radio 4
Broadcasting House
London
W1A 1AA
Tel: 071-580 4468

That's Life
BBC Television Centre
Wood Lane
London W12 8QT
Tel: 071-743 8000

Watchdog
BBC Television Centre
Wood Lane
London W12 8QT
Tel: 071-743 8000

Panorama
BBC Television Centre
Wood Lane
London W12 8QT
Tel: 071-743 8000

Rough Justice
BBC Television Centre
Wood Lane
London W12 8QT
Tel: 071-743 8000

World In Action
Granada Television
Granada Television Centre
Manchester
Lancashire M60 9EA
Tel: 061-832 7211

Dispatches
Channel 4
60 Charlotte Street
London W1P 2AX
Tel: 071-631 4000

11

Complaints

The press, radio and television provide an indespensable service in any democratic society, as the media is often the sole provider of information. Clearly, access to information is a fundamental prerequisite for any public participation in the decision-making processes of a free and democratic society. The media, therefore, possesses a huge responsibility to the communities it serves, and it is the reponsibility of those of us who use that information – and also the responsibility of those of us who help to make the news – to keep the media under constant scrutiny. With a few notorious exceptions, most newspaper publishers and broadcasters are sensitive to complaints and praise, and as in many other spheres of life the public is able to influence decisions at a very senior level.

Complaining about the activities of those publishers and broadcasters, though, is not a straightforward issue, as it may well depend upon a number of factors. For example, are you the direct vicitim of some erroneous reporting, or merely a by-stander? Was the alleged fault actually a reporting error or did you simply disagree with a conclusion or opinion? Each individual complaint, of course, has to be judged according to its merit. But this chapter outlines the different approaches, and various formal bodies, that exist to pursue complaints of any substance.

Minor complaints

Many complaints are relatively minor, and can be resolved by contacting the appropriate editor directly and putting your case to her. For example, a local newspaper may print a factual inaccuracy about your organization in a news story. You will obviously want the error corrected so that the public has access to accurate information, and you will also want that correction published sooner rather than later. There can be few reasons for an editor to object to such a request except, possibly, that she may view the publication of a correction as something of an embarrassment. Alternatively, you may disagree with an opinion piece in the newspaper's editorial columns, and consider the editor to be totally misguided in her views. In any event, you should be able to make your views publicly known.

Factual errors – newspapers
If a newspaper prints a factual error then the key objective is to get the error corrected without delay, preferably in the next edition. It may be appropriate to telephone the news desk and raise the matter with the news editor. However, it may be better to write a letter to the letters column giving the correct information. One of the advantages of a letter is that the letters column is widely read, and you will communicate to a much larger audience. On the other hand, a correction will probably be no more than a short paragraph at the bottom of a news page. Few people will read it, and fewer still will really take any notice of it. As we have already seen, some editors receive relatively little in the way of contributions to the letters page, and the editor may well view your complaint to be an appropriate matter to raise in that column. By using the letters column you will have the opportunity of expanding on the subject of the complaint, and you can instantly increase the amount of publicity generated by your cause.

You should also attempt to establish *why* this mistake has occurred. Was your briefing material accurate? Did your press release and backgrounder provide all the necessary information?

If you get the opportunity to talk to the journalists involved in the production of the erroneous article then this may encourage them to avoid making similar mistakes in the future. Serious errors in newspapers, both local and national and which the editor is unwilling to correct, can be referred to the Press Complaints Commission (see page 131).

Factual errors – radio

If a radio station broadcasts an error then simply phone through to the producer of that programme asking for a swift correction to be broadcast. This is particularly appropriate if the error is broadcast in a live magazine programme. An error in a radio news bulletin can be corrected so that subsequent bulletins do not repeat the same mistake. Most local radio stations broadcast phone-in programmes where the public is invited to comment and debate on live radio, and this may give you direct access to the airwaves. If serious complaints against radio stations are unresolved then there are two bodies to whom complaints can be referred: the Radio Authority (see page 135) handles complaints about commercial radio stations; and the Broadcasting Complaints Commission (see page 134) deals with complaints against BBC radio stations.

Factual errors – television

There is little that can be done in the short term about correcting factual errors broadcast on television, as most television output is pre-recorded. If an error is broadcast then the first course of action is to telephone the appropriate station and make your complaint known to the duty officer. Every television station has a duty officer available throughout its transmission times – as do the national radio stations – who will log all complaints, comments and praise from the public. The stations are obliged to log all such calls, and they are routinely referred to the programme makers. If you want your complaint to be formally investigated then it will be necessary to write to the director of programming at the station setting out your complaint and asking for it to be investigated. If the investigation is unsatisfactory from your

point of view then it is possible to complain to one of the
three complaints bodies that handle television complaints: the
Broadcasting Complaints Commission (see page 134); the
Broadcasting Standards Council (see page 135); or the
Independent Television Commission (see pages 135–136).

Differences of opinion

If you feel that your complaint is not one of fact but one of
opinion, then you should consider ways by which you can
fight like with like – why not try to obtain publicity for free
and make your feelings known? With newspapers you might
try to use the letters column or approach the editor with a
proposal for a feature article. On the radio there are phone-ins
and access programmes; and television stations have similar
facilities for the public to put their points of view.

Major complaints

A number of official bodies exist to process complaints against
newspapers, radio stations and television programmes. The
complaints procedures are available for public use, and they
do not require any fees to be paid. However, there are two
important considerations that need to be taken into account
before using these procedures: firstly, some media executives
will feel very bitter about any member of the public using
formal complaints procedures. It has been said that this
particularly applies to some editors of local or regional
newspapers, who are in a position to refuse to publish any
further articles about you or your organization. Remember,
they have absolutely no obligation whatsoever to report any
issue or event that they choose to ignore. Therefore, consider
carefully the potential benefits and hazards of lodging a
formal complaint against your local newspaper.

The second consideration is that any formal complaint will
generate quite a lot of paperwork which will take up time;
only instigate a complaint if you are willing to see the matter
through.

Press Complaints Commission

The complaints body for investigating and adjudicating in complaints against both national and local newspapers – and magazines – is the Press Complaints Commission. This body replaced the Press Council in 1991. The Commission's Code of Practice states that in the first instance the complaints should be put in writing directly to the editor of the accused publication. He or she should then be given at least seven days in which to respond to your complaint. If the editor does not respond, or the response is unacceptable from your point of view, then the matter may be referred to the Press Complaints Commission. The Commission publishes a number of guides on dealing with complaints against a newspaper, and the general guidance notes and Code of Practice include the following provisions:

- **Accuracy:** the Press Complaints Commission requires newspapers not to publish material that is 'inaccurate, misleading or distorted'. If such material is published then the code requires it to be corrected promptly and 'with due prominence'. It requires an apology to be published if appropriate, and newspapers are required to 'distinguish between comment, conjecture and fact'.

- **Privacy:** intrusion into the private life of an individual is 'not generally acceptable' and publication of material gained through intrusion can only be justified in the public interest. This covers four eventualities: (i) detecting or exposing crime or serious misdemeanour; (ii) detecting or exposing serious anti-social conduct; (iii) protecting public health and safety; and (iv) preventing the public from being misled by some statement or action of that individual.

- **Misrepresentation:** the code states that 'journalists should not generally obtain or seek to obtain information or pictures through misrepresentation or subterfuge'. It also prevents journalists from obtaining information or pictures through intimidation or harassment.

- **Discrimination:** the Code of Practice requires the press to avoid 'prejudicial or pejorative reference to a person's race, colour, religion, sex or sexual orientation or to any physical or mental illness or handicap'. Reference to these matters should be avoided by the press unless they are directly relevant to the story.

- **Right of reply:** the Code states that 'a fair opportunity for reply to inaccuracies should be given to individuals or organizations when reasonably called for'.

- The Code of Practice also covers other headings including: intrusion into grief or shock; interviewing and photographing children; victims of crime; payment for articles; innocent friends or relatives; and hospitals. A copy of the Code of Practice is available without charge directly from the Commission.

The Press Complaints Commission can be contacted at:

1 Salisbury Square
London EC4Y 8AE
Tel: 071-353 1248
Fax: 071-353 8355

National Union of Journalists Code of Conduct

Many journalists, both on newspapers and in the broadcasting field, are members of the National Union of Jornalists. They are bound by a Code of Conduct, and can be disciplined by the NUJ if they act outside of the code. The code states:

1. A journalist has a duty to maintain the highest professional and ethical standards.

2. A journalist shall at all times defend the principle of the freedom of the press and other media in relation to the collection of information and the expression of comment and criticism. He/she shall strive to eliminate distortion, news suppression and censorship.

3. A journalist shall strive to ensure that the information he/she disseminates is fair and accurate, avoid the expression of comment and conjecture as established fact and falsification by distortion, selection or mis-representation.

4. A journalist shall rectify promptly any harmful inaccuracies, ensure that correction and apologies receive due prominence and afford the right of reply to persons criticized when the issue is of sufficient importance.

5. A journalist shall obtain information, photographs and illustrations only by straightforward means. The use of other means can be justified only by overriding considerations of the public interest. The journalist is entitled to exercise a personal conscientious objection to the use of such means.

6. Subject to the justification by overriding considerations of the public interest, a journalist shall do nothing which entails intrusion into private grief and distress.

7. A journalist shall protect confidential sources of information.

8. A journalist shall not accept bribes nor shall he/she allow other inducements to influence the performance of his/her professional duties.

9. A journalist shall not lend himself/herself to the distortion or suppression of the truth because of advertising or other considerations.

10. A journalist shall only mention a person's race, colour, creed, illegitimacy, marital status (or lack of it), gender

or sexual orientation if this information is strictly relevant. A journalist shall neither originate nor process material which encourages discrimination on any of the above-mentioned grounds.

11. A journalist shall not take private advantage of information gained in the course of his/her duties, before the information is public knowledge.

12. A journalist shall not by way of statement, voice or appearance endorse by advertisement any commercial product or service save for the promotion of his/her own work or of the medium by which he/she is employed.

The National Union of Journalists also has guidelines on race and journalists; and on reporting racist organizations. Further information about the Code of Practice and the Guidelines are available from:

The General Secretary
National Union of Journalists
314 Gray's Inn Road
London WC1X 8DP
Tel: 071-278 7916

Broadcasting Complaints Commission

The Commission is empowered to investigate complaints only if they fall into either of two categories: (i) unjust or unfair treatment in radio or television programmes actually broadcast or included in a licensed cable or satellite programme service; (ii) unwarranted infringement of privacy in, or in connection with the obtaining of material included in, such programmes. Complaints can generally be lodged only by an individual or organization that has a direct interest in the programme or event complained of. Complaints can be made about any programme on BBC TV, BBC Radio, BBC World Service, Independent Radio, ITV, Channel 4, S4C and cable or satellite programmes. This includes advertisements and teletext transmissions. The Commission is unable to consider complaints about: the depiction of sex or violence; bad language or bad taste; background music; or programme scheduling. Further information about the Commission, and copies of its complaints form, are available from:

The Secretary
The Broadcasting Complaints Commission
35–37 Grosvenor Gardens
London SW1W 0BS
Tel: 071-630 1966

The Broadcasting Standards Council
This Council monitors the portrayal of violence, sex and related matters of taste and decency (such as bad language or the treatment of disasters). It publishes a lengthy and detailed Code of Practice that is available from:

Broadcasting Standards Council
5–8 The Sanctuary
London SW1P 3JS
Tel: 071-233 0544
Fax: 071-233 0397

Radio Authority
Whereas the Broadcasting Complaints Commission deals only with complaints from individuals directly affected by individual broadcasts, the Radio Authority considers complaints from the public about all aspects of programming, advertising and transmission on commercial radio stations. The Radio Authority is available at:

70 Brompton Road
London SW3 1EY
Tel: 071-581 2888

Independent Television Commission
Similarly, the ITC can deal with a broad range of complaints

from the public about programming, advertising and transmission of all Channel 3 stations and the Channel 4 output. Details of the ITC's work is available from:

70 Brompton Road
London SW3 1EY
Tel: 071-584 7011

Hard News

This is a television programme periodically broadcast on Channel 4 and which examines the behaviour of the press and allegations of misconduct. *Hard News* attempts to provide victims of press harassment with the right to reply, and can be contacted at:

Hard News
Kenilworth House
80 Margaret Street
London W1N 7HB
Tel: 071-636 4444

Advertising Standards Authority

Any advertisement that appears in a newspaper or magazine must be accurate and truthful. If an advertisement is inaccurate or untruthful, or otherwise offensive or illegal, you can complain to the Advertising Standards Authority (ASA). The ASA is an independent body responsible for policing the strict standards that apply to adverts for drugs, tobacco and alcohol – as well as the general British Code of Advertising Practice that applies to all other advertisements. The ASA also publishes a monthly bulletin of complaints that the organization has considered during the previous month. If you think that an advertisement is misleading, offensive or illegal you should write to the ASA giving full details of the advert and your reasons for complaint, and if possible a copy of the advertisement. Details of the work of the ASA is available from:

Advertising Standards Authority
Brook House
2–16 Torrington Place
London WC1E 7HN
Tel: 071-580 5555
Fax: 071-631 3051

Libel and slander

Anyone is entitled to protection and to seek redress against unfair and malicious attack. A newspaper or broadcasting organization that damages anyone's reputation can be sued in the High Court for libel or slander. Reporters and editors are usually very cautious about publishing comments that might be defamatory, and often consult specialist libel lawyers to check articles that are in doubt. Indeed, some national newspapers employ staff lawyers solely for the purpose of checking material for libel. If the defamatory remark was spoken then it is slander; if it is printed in a newspaper or magazine then it is libel. The law of defamation is extremely difficult to prove, and even individual cases that appear to be similar can produce very different results in court. Never enter into libel or slander legal proceedings lightly as they will be very costly, and Legal Aid is not available for such cases.

For a libel action to stand any chance of success you must prove that the statement was slanderous or that the article was libellous. It is also necessary to prove that the offending article was circulated or broadcast to a 'third party' – that is, almost anybody else, which will apply if the article was published in a newspaper or broadcast by a radio or television station. However, even if those conditions apply there are still the complex legal defences of justification, privilege and fair comment. Libel and slander cases will almost always need the services of a lawyer, and the lawyer will usually require payment. However, one possible compromise would be to pay a solicitor to send the newspaper a sharp letter. This may generate an apology from the offender, and they may be a little more cautious when dealing with you in future.

Media monitoring

This is a relatively new activity involving the undertaking of research into the amount of coverage given by newspapers or broadcasters to a particular subject. For example, the main political parties, Conservative and Labour, closely monitor the amount of coverage each receives on a particular story. The one with less coverage will then cry 'foul' and claim that the newspaper or broadcaster is biased in favour of the other party.

Media monitoring does play a useful role in monitoring the attitudes and policies of media organizations. If you feel that the media consistently misrepresents or under-represents your cause or organization then you will need to gather evidence to back up your claim. A monitoring exercise can be as large or small as you can accommodate. You might simply want to scan coverage of a single event, or examine specific cases of misrepresentation over a longer period. Examples of media monitoring include a one-week monitor of one particular daily newspaper for sexist comments, to a two-week national press monitoring analysis of newspaper items covering gay and lesbian issues.

Remember, though, that media monitoring is hard work, and requires access to various resources, including video recorders, radio/tape recorders and copies of all the newspapers involved.

How to get publicity for free – complaints checklist

- Be well prepared. Make sure you clearly understand what you are complaining about, and why you are complaining. Keep your complaint polite and confident rather than abusive.
- Respond to an offensive item or programme speedily by making a telephone call and then following it up with a letter if you feel the complaint warrants it. Give the media organization

a reasonable period in which to process your complaint.

- If necessary, report the matter to the appropriate watchdog organization. But remember that this can be a time-consuming activity and that results are not always immediate.
- Remember that in a free and democratic society the media itself is often a watchdog of the activities of official bodies and individuals. The public has to be the watchdog of the media.

12

Help!

Obtaining publicity for free is within the grasp of most
organizations and individuals. However, there are times when
outside advice or assistance may be needed; for example, a
small community group may need to find access to inexpen-
sive duplicating or photocopying facilities for the production
of a press release. There will almost certainly be someone in
your neighbourhood who will be able to provide you with
advice or assistance.

Resources

Access to cheap or cost-effective copying facilities and
stationery will be necessary for individuals or organizations
that are operating on very limited budgets. Such facilities may
be available through a local community association or trade
union resource centre. Ask at your local library or local
Citizens Advice Bureau. Some educational establishments may
offer reduced-cost copying facilities for community groups.
Check to see if your community has an umbrella organization
for voluntary groups, such as a Council for Voluntary Service
(CVS). They may be able to advise you about resources.

Courses

An increasing number of media-related courses are now available to anyone who is prepared to pay the appropriate fee. From beginners' journalism to advanced sub-editing and television interviewing, courses are offered by a wide range of consultancies and academic bodies involved in media work, and are often advertised in the Monday supplement of the *Guardian*. But beware. If you choose to go on a course make sure that you check it out thoroughly, as some of the courses offered by commercial organizations are seen as being opportunist rip-offs. Your local adult education centre, technical college or other educational establishments are likely to provide affordable courses with professional tutors and access to a wide range of facilities.

Journalists

As a publicist it is worthwhile to make contact with journalists in your area; indeed, unless you are hugely unsuccessful as a publicist you will certainly establish some contacts. It may also be beneficial to develop links with journalists through local branches of the journalist's trade unions. As trade unionists, journalists do often take an interest in local issues. For example, the Whiteoak Action Campaign and the related issues mentioned in Chapter 2 should be of considerable interest to the local journalists, and Gary Bysouth could benefit by offering to address a meeting of the local branch. This will give him an opportunity to brief accurately the reporters about the campaign and background issues, and at the same time he will get to know the journalists who will be covering the campaign in the weeks and months ahead. Those links will be particularly useful if you find yourself in dispute with the editor or proprietor of the local newspaper or radio station, and you can then also hear about new access programmes, changes of policy and the like. The three main trade unions for journalists are:

British Association of Journalists
97 Fleet Street
London EC4Y 1DH
Tel: 071-353 3003

Institute of Journalists
2 Dock Offices
Surrey Quay
Lower Road
London SE16 2XL
Tel: 071-252 1187

National Union of Journalists
314 Gray's Inn Road
London WC1X 8DP
Tel: 071-278 7916

Writers' groups

As a publicist you may wish to develop your writing skills by joining a local writers' group. The type and quality of such groups will vary from area to area, and will often be dominated by individuals interested in poetry and other forms of creative writing. However, they may also include freelance journalists and published authors, and have the prospect of providing useful resources and assistance to a local publicist. The following organizations may be able to steer you in the direction of writing groups or courses in your area:

The Society of Authors
84 Drayton Gardens
London SW10 9SB
Tel: 071-373 6642

Writers' Guild of Great Britain
430 Edgware Road
London W2 1EH
Tel: 071-723 8074

Directory of Writers Circles
Jill Dick
Oldacre
Horderns Park Road
Chapel-en-le-Frith
Derbyshire SK12 6SY

Also, a list of specialist writers' groups is published in the *Writers' and Artists' Yearbook* (A&C Black) and other directories that are usually available for inspection in reference libraries.

Censorship

A number of organizations are concerned about censorship of the printed word and programmes for broadcast, and should be approached directly for further information:

Article 19 is an international human rights organization working impartially to promote the right of freedom of expression and information.

90 Borough High Street
London SE1 1LL
Tel: 071-403 4822
Fax: 071-403 1943

Charter 88 campaigns for constitutional reform in the United Kingdom, including a written constitution, a bill of rights and electoral reform.

3 Pine Street
London EC1R 0JH
Tel: 071–833 1988
Fax: 071–833 5895

Campaign for Freedom of Information is the main anti-State secrecy campaign group, and is pressing for the Official Secrets Act to be repealed and replaced with a Freedom of Information Act.

88 Old Street
London EC1V 9AR
Tel: 071-253 2445

Index on Censorship is a magazine that fights censorship worldwide by printing the work of censored poets, playwrights, journalists, authors and publishers.

39c Highbury Place
London N5 1QP
Tel: 071-359 0161
Fax: 071-354 8665

Liberty, formerly the National Council for Civil Liberties, is committed to the defence and extension of civil liberties in the UK, and to promoting the rights and freedoms recognized by international law.

21 Tabard Street
London SE1 4LA
Tel: 071-403 3888
Fax: 071-407 5354

Statewatch is a civil rights bulletin and on-line database monitoring the State, police, the security and intelligence agencies and the like.

PO Box 1516
London N16 0EW
Tel: 081-802 1882
Fax: 081-880 1727

13

International

It is somewhat rare for local news stories to attract the attention
of the international press and broadcast media, and rarer still for
them to break as news stories in other countries. But there will
be exceptions to this general rule. For example, if your town or
city is twinned with towns and cities in other countries – as is
often the case – then the newspapers and radio and television
stations in those communities may take an interest in the events
and activities in your community. The type of news events that
might achieve some level of educational coverage could include:

- A factory in England supplies industrial parts to a
  major German car manufacturer. The English factory
  receives a 'Queen's Award For Industry' accolade for
  its record export achievements, and the factory
  announces its success by issuing a press release. The
  factory also thinks that it would be appropriate to
  inform the local media in the German town where
  the car manufacturer is located. The English factory
  could also send the press release to the German trade
  press – those are the specialist magazines and other
  periodicals that relate to a particular subject or
  industry. This type of publicity will boost the image
  of the company – and might even attract further
  business – by simply drawing up a mailing list of
  appropriate media organizations.

● A Scottish seaside town is 'twinned' with several towns and cities abroad – in the United States of America, Scandinavia and elsewhere in Europe. Environmental campaigners in the Scottish town discover that beach pollution in the area from local factories and other sources is far in excess of European Community regulations, but the British government has no plans to enforce those regulations or to make local offenders clean up their act. The environmental pressure group launches a campaign to put pressure on the British government to deal with the pollution, and the campaign includes the issuing of a press release to make the findings public. The press release could be sent to local newspapers and broadcasters in the twinned towns, and include a call for those communities to put pressure on the British authorities to take action. This can be done, for example, by encouraging individuals to write protest letters to the British Embassy, or lobbying their own MEP to put pressure on the offending government.

Finding the foreign press

Lists of newspapers and broadcasting organizations throughout the world are published in the two main media directories, *Willings Press Guide* and *Benns Media Directory*. These reference books will enable you to draw up a press mailing list for the specific areas that you have in mind. Many foreign news organizations have offices or correspondents in London, such as *Der Spiegel* or the Australian Broadcasting Service. They are listed in the London *Yellow Pages* under 'Newspapers and Magazines' or 'Broadcasting Services'. The representatives of foreign media organizations closely monitor our own newspapers and radio and television services for appropriate 'leads' on stories that they in turn pick up for their own use. Also, if your town or city is 'twinnned' with those in other countries then your local district or county council might employ a Twinning Officer. He or she may be able to give you useful advice and contacts. Check with the Town Hall or County Council Headquarters.

Translations

The British are notorious for speaking only English, but most foreign newspapers or radio and television stations will understand a press release or backgrounder sent to them in English. If possible, though, have your press release translated into the appropriate language. It would be particularly appropriate to send the material out in English, French and German as these are the three main international languages recognized in the so-called 'developed' world.

14

Do-it-yourself publicity

One guaranteed method of obtaining publicity is to publish your own leaflets, reports, newsletters or news bulletins. The key advantage of publishing your own publicity material is that you have complete editorial control over that material. In other words, you can say anything you want – within the constraints of the law, of course. The obvious disadvantage, however, is that you have to produce the material yourself, and pay for it to be printed, so it is not a way of obtaining publicity for free. But for a group or organization that plans to be active on a long-term basis – and which has the financial resources – such material may complement any publicity obtained for free in the press or on the airwaves. An important word of warning, though: any organization will instantly see the benefits of, say, producing a regular newsletter. After all, a monthly or bi-monthly newsletter will keep members and supporters informed of the organization's activities; provide a 'what's on' diary; allow individual members to air their views; act as a means of co-ordinating the group's work; and so on. What is often overlooked, though, is the amount of sheer hard work involved in such an enterprise. Although producing your own publicity material can add to the prestige of your organization, to announce that you plan to publish a regular newsletter and then to fail to come up with the goods can be a potentially damaging embarrassment.

The important issues to bear in mind when planning any do-it-yourself publicity campaign include:

People power

The publication of regular publicity material of some depth, such as a newsletter, will require a number of people to undertake planning the publication; research and information gathering; writing articles; typing up the text; producing artwork; printing the publication – or obtaining printing quotes and liaising with printers; and carrying out the distribution.

This will be an enormous job, and anyone contemplating such a task should really consider whether the organization has sufficient individuals with sufficient commitment to enable it to take place effectively.

Skills

What skills do members or supporters of your organization have? Are there people who can write short but interesting news items in a simple conversational style? Are there any artists or designers who can produce simple artwork such as logos, or help with the layout of a leaflet or bulletin? What about distribution? Once you have produced your own publicity material, how are you going to get it to your intended audience? You need to conduct a very thorough examination of the skills and commitment of the other people involved in your organization.

Resources

The most important resource needed in the production of publicity material is money. Unless you have access to completely free printing and production facilities – which will apply to very few groups – there will be some cost involved in the production of the publications. You will need to obtain competitive quotes from a number of different printers. Is there a resource centre in your area that can provide cheap printing or photocopying facilities? Do you know anybody who will let you have access to a word processor or to desk-top publishing equipment?

Is it worth it?

Before committing yourself and your group's resources to any do-it-yourself publishing activities, you should consider carefully the potential benefit of undertaking that activity and ask yourself the seemingly obvious question: is it worth it? Who is the intended audience of your proposed publicity material? Why do you need a leaflet or bulletin to communicate the information to those people – could that be achieved more easily and effectively by issuing a press release to the local media? What are the cost implications of your do-it-yourself publicity plans? Does your group have the financial resources to pay for that type of publicity material and, even if it does, could such funds be better used by the organization in other ways? You should give very careful consideration to any publicity ideas before going ahead.

Newsletters

Although we have already considered some of the problems and pitfalls that can arise from taking on the major task of publishing a newsletter, it can also be a relatively simple and straightforward task. For example, take another look at the sample backgrounder document shown in Chapter 3 on pages 50–51. The same simple techniques and limited resources can be applied to produce a very simple but effective news bulletin. Note that the backgrounder was produced on a conventional manual typewriter and two sheets of A4 paper. Each paragraph can be a brief article that updates the readership on a particular aspect of the organization and its work. The text is simply typed across the page and given a straightforward headline. Artwork is unnecessary, although the impact of a bulletin or newsletter is increased if the front page is printed or photocopied on to headed notepaper or on to a specially produced masthead (which is the block at the top of most newspapers and magazines that bears the name of the publication). Such a newsletter or bulletin can be any length, from one side of A4 paper through to several pages with text printed on both sides, and can be easily produced by photocopying. Therefore a regular news bulletin or simple newsletter can be within the grasp of many small voluntary and campaigning organizations.

The Kent Gay Action Newsletter shown below is a good example of a cheaply produced but effective bulletin. Although produced on a stencil duplicator it reads like a newspaper.

KENT GAY ACTION

KENT'S BEST BUY
FOR GAY news
+ INFORMATION

NEWSLETTER 10p

AUGUST 1982   :MONTHLY: ISSUE NUMBER 6

PAPER REJECTS HELP-LINE ADVERT

Within days of the launch of Britain's newest gay help-line last month, there came the first setback in its attempts to get itself known to the people of mid-Kent. This happened when the Chatham News, which claims to have the largest weekly circulation in the county, rejected a paid advertisement from Medway and Maidstone Gay Switchboard.

The advert would have read: "Homosexual women and men - for information and advice phone Gay Switchboard. Medway 826925 every Thursday and Friday, 7.30-9.30pm only. " The paper's Advertisement Manager, Mike Souter, thanked Switchboard for the advert, but returned their cheque saying "Unfortunately it is not the policy of our company to accept advertisements of this nature".

READ IT FIRST IN KGA N E W S L E T T E R

New magazine out in January

Britain is to get a new national gay magazine in January next year. Plans are that it will be published three times a year and called Resonance. It will be produced by one of the sub-groups of Gay Workshops.

After their meeting on July 29 Philip Payne told KGA Newsletter that the group wanted to make the magazine accessible to as many people as possible. A low cover price was one way of doing this, but was not enough by itself. Language is seen as
CONTINUED ON BACK PAGE-.

'Racist' at Gayfest

Among the delights at this year's Gay Festival is a speaker who is both racist and sexist. Capital Gay (30 July) says Percy Barnsby will address a 2½ hour meeting on Mithras Shinto, which he calls the 'gay religion'. He talks of Asian and African people as being interested only in copulation; he teaches that lesbianism is a childish escape from responsibility. Men who misuse the 'phallic power' may become women in the next life. Gay News will no longer take his advertisements.

A Switchboard spokesperson told KGA Newsletter "We are not totally surprised by the response of the paper, as it is not noted for taking a liberal line on any issue. However, I think our hopes had been raised when the Chatham News carried a small news item, including the help-line's number, on 2 July".

Among the factors which led the service to want to advertise in the paper were its high circulation in the Medway Towns combined with a relatively low price. The Switchboard spokesperson told us that a single insertion of the wording, set out above, would cost £1.98 a week, and it would also appear in the personal column of the Chatham Standard at no extra cost. The same advert in the Kent Messenger, we are told, would cost over three times as much - £6.50 a week.

"Personally I am not very optimistic about the possibility of the News being persuaded to carry the advert", the Switchboard spokesperson told KGA Newsletter. "But we will carry on trying for some time yet", they continued, "as the service is failing if it is not reaching new gay people".
○ SWITCHBOARD - THE SUCCESSES, SEE P.3

On the other hand, not everybody gets it right first time:

SOUTHWARK'S
ISSUE 1
CREDIT UNION NEWS

The Southwark Credit Union Development Agency (SCUDA) grew out of 'faith in the city and Inner City Regeneration Programme' and is funded by the London Borough of Southwark, the Inner Area Programme and the Church Urban Fund.

It was set up in 1989 to bring economic benefits to residents and employees in the London Borough of Southwark.

The Agency employs 4 staff:

Mr Roy McLeod (Co-ordinator)
Mrs Joan Drane (Sec/Admin)
Miss Connie Gbidi (Development Off)
Mrs Chris Cobham. (Development Off)

The Agency is also managed by a Board of Directors:

Rev. Canon. Peter Challen (South London Industrial Mission.), Mr Paul Williams (Camberwell Credit Union), Mr Peter Bussey (Association of British Credit Unions Limited), Ms Ros Dillon (Southwark Money Advice Centre), Mr Steve Provins (Southwark Council Employees Credit Union) Mr Bill Yoxall (Southwark Council)

SCUDA has been set up to promote the 2 existing credit unions (Camberwell Credit Union and the Southwark Council Employees Credit Union), establish new credit unions and make credit union benefits and services available to all residents and employees in Southwark and to help address the cause of multiple debt and denial of reasonable credit facilities which drive people to lenders charging exorbitant rates of interest.

The Agency is funded for a period of 4 years of which it has another 2 years to operate.

SCUDA is hoping that many people will take advantage of the services being provided before its funding runs out.

However, the Agency is looking to seek other means of funding to continue its services.

WHAT IS A CREDIT UNION

Credit unions are saving and loans co-operatives and operate for the benefit of its members.

It is a non-profit making organisation providing people with low cost loans for helping with big bills, e.g gas, electricity, cars decorating, you name it. They are also an easy painless way to save for a holiday, wedding, christmas, whatever.

Credit unions can be set up in community centres/groups, churches, Tenants Associations, clubs, organisations.

Credit unions are set up and run by the members. Only members and their

The National Federation of Community Organizations publishes an excellent booklet, *Making news – producing a community newspaper*, by Barbara Lowndes. It is available from the NFCO, 8 Upper Street, Islington, London N1 0PQ.

Leaflets

A leaflet is a very brief published statement about an immediate aspect of a campaign's work. It will usually have a clear audience in mind – such as residents in a specific neighbourhood or those attending a particular public meeting. Leaflets should contain the minimum number of words to convey the intended message, and should also provide other important details such as how to contact the organization for further information. For examples of leaflets that are published by a wide range of local and national organizations you should call in to your local reference library. Samples of leaflets published by other bodies will give you an idea of the size and style that can be used effectively by your group.

Reports

It is also possible that your group or organization will wish to publish details of its research into areas of its activity. For example, a local branch of an environmental pressure group may wish to put together a report of its evidence into a particular pollution hazard; or a women's group may have conducted research into sex discrimination at the workplace and wishes to make its findings known. Such material can be very potent when press released to the local media, but must be presented clearly. Before producing your own reports it would be worthwhile closely examining those published by other organizations to gain an idea of an effective style and format.

Miscellaneous

Given the financial resources, it is possible to get almost any type of publicity material printed, from small leaflets to posters of any size. Poster hoardings in prominent public positions can be rented by the hour, and it is possible to rent space on the side of buses on which to display posters and other forms of advertising material. Loudspeaker cars – often seen at the time of parliamentary and local government elections – can be used to spread the word (but check with the local police first to make sure that no local by-laws prohibit such activities), and the proverbial sandwich board is a well tried and trusted means of communication. A little lateral thinking will enable you to come up with methods of getting your message across at little, if any, expense.

How to get publicity for free – DIY publicity checklist

- Make sure that your group or organization is aware of the time it takes to produce effective and detailed publicity material such as newsletters.
- Clearly assess the costs involved in the production of any paid-for publicity material, and also the skills and resources that are available to you for free.
- Look at alternative ways of getting your message across to your intended audience at considerably less cost and using fewer resources – such as a press release.

Appendix 1

National newspapers

There are eleven daily national newspapers and ten Sunday national newspapers in the United Kingdom. The circulation figures apply to October 1992.

Daily Mirror
Holborn Circus
London EC1P 1DQ
Tel: 071–353 0246
Circulation: 3,601,374

The Sun
1 Virginia Street
London E1 9XP
Tel: 071–782 4000
Circulation: 3,629,893

Daily Mail
Northcliffe House
2 Derry Street
Kensington
London W8 5TS
Tel: 071–938 6000
Circulation: 1,744,251

Daily Express
Ludgate House
245 Blackfriars Road
London SE1 9UX
Tel: 071–928 8000
Circulation: 1,564,553

Daily Star
Ludgate House
245 Blackfriars Road
London SE1 9UX
Tel: 071–928 8000
Circulation: 810,210

Today
1 Pennington Street
London E1 9XN
Tel: 071–782 5000
Circulation: 563,234

Daily Telegraph
Peterborough Court
South Quay
181 Marsh Wall
London E14 9SR
Tel: 071–538 5000
Circulation: 1,047,762

Guardian
119 Farringdon Road
London EC1R 3ER
Tel: 071–278 2332
Circulation: 414,570

Independent
40 City Road
London EC1Y 2DB
Tel: 071–253 1222
Circulation: 375,942

The Times
1 Pennington Street
London E1 9XN
Tel: 071–782 5000
Circulation: 377,995

Financial Times
Number One
Southwark Bridge
London SE1 9HL
Tel: 071–873 3000
Circulation: 289,352

News of the World
1 Virginia Street
London E1 9XR
Tel: 071–782 4000
Circulation: 4,797,092

Sunday Mirror
Holborn Circus
London EC1P 1DQ
Tel: 071–353 0246
Circulation: 2,749,029

The People
Holborn Circus
London EC1P 1DQ
Tel: 071–353 0246
Circulation: 2,110,495

Mail on Sunday
Northcliffe House
2 Derry Street
Kensington
London W8 5TS
Tel: 071–938 6000
Circulation: 1,968,281

Sunday Express
Ludgate House
245 Blackfriars Road
London SE1 9UX
Tel: 071–928 8000
Circulation: 1,802,719

Sunday Sport
Marten House
39–47 East Road
London N1 6AH
Tel: 071–251 2544
Circulation: 304,010

Sunday Times
1 Pennington Street
London E1 9XW
Tel: 071–782 5000
Circulation: 1,184,909

Sunday Telegraph
Peterborough Court
South Quay
181 Marsh Wall
London E14 9SR
Tel: 071–782 5000
Circulation: 590,336

Observer
Chelsea Bridge House
Queenstown Road
London SW8 4NN
Tel: 071–627 0700
Circulation: 527,931

Independent on Sunday
40 City Road
London EC1B 2DB
Tel: 071–253 1222
Circulation: 417,682

News agencies

There are two main news agencies in the United Kingdom: the Press Association, which services news stories for newspapers throughout this country; and Reuters, which deals with overseas stories.

Press Association
85 Fleet Street
London EC4P 4BE
Tel: 071–353 7440

Reuters
85 Fleet Street
London EC4P 4AJ
Tel: 071–250 1122

Appendix 2

National and regional television

BBC Television
Television Centre
Wood Lane
London W12 8QT
Tel: 071–743 8000

BSkyB
6 Centaurs Business Park
Grant Way
Isleworth
Middlesex TW7 5QD
Tel: 071–782 3000

Channel Four Television
60 Charlotte Street
London W1P 2AX
Tel: 071–631 4444

Good Morning Television
The London Television
  Centre
London SE1 9LT
Tel: 071–827 7000

Good Morning Television
branch studios:

Lyndon Court
Queen Street
Belfast
County Antrim BT2 7GE
Tel: (0232) 333326

First House Productions
1 Sutton Street
Holloway Head
Birmingham
West Midlands B1 1PE
Tel: 021–666 6532

Argyle House
Castlebridge
5–12 Cowbridge Road East
Cardiff
South Glamorgan CF1 3AB
Tel: (0222) 340920

Block 2 East
5 Northgate
Cowcaddens
Glasgow
Strathclyde G4 0BB
Tel: 041–331 2200

5 Tabley Court
Stamford Street
Altrincham
Cheshire WA14 1EZ
Tel: 061–928 7414

Ground Floor
Crestina House
Archbold Terrace
Jesmond
Newcastle upon Tyne
Tyne & Wear NE2 1DB
Tel: 091–281 9666

28 Broadway
Peterborough
Cambridgeshire PE1 1RS
Tel: (0733) 896886

**Independent Television
  News (ITN)**
200 Gray's Inn Road
London WC1X 8XZ
Tel: 071–833 3000

Anglia Television
Anglia House
Norwich
Norfolk NR1 3JG
Tel: (0603) 615151

**Anglia Television
branch studios:**

4 Jesus Lane
Cambridge
Cambridgeshire CB5 8BA
Tel: (0223) 467076

64–68 New London Road
Chelmsford
Essex CM2 0YU
Tel: (0245) 357676

16 Park Street
Luton
Bedfordshire LU1 2DP
Tel: (0582) 29666

77b Abington Street
Northampton
Northamptonshire NN1 2BH
Tel: (0604) 24343

28 The Broadway
Peterborough
Cambridgeshire PE1 1RS
Tel: (0733) 46677

Hubbard House
Civic Drive
Ipswich
Suffolk IP1 2QA
Tel: (0473) 226157

Unit 14
The Food Centre
409 Secklow Gate East
Milton Keynes
Buckinghamshire MK9 3NT
Tel: (0908) 691660

Border Television
Television Centre
Carlisle
Cumbria CA1 3NT
Tel: (0228) 25101

Carlton Television
101 St Martin's Lane
London WC2N 4AZ
Tel: 071–240 4000

Central
Central House
Broad Street
Birmingham
West Midlands B1 2JP
Tel: 021–643 9898

Central
branch studios:

East Midlands Television
   Centre
Lenton Lane
Nottingham
Nottinghamshire NG7 2NA
Tel: (0602) 863322

Unit 9
Windrush Court
Abingdon Business Park
Abingdon
Oxfordshire OX14 1SA
Tel: (0235) 554123

Channel Television
The Television Centre
La Pouquelaye
St Helier
Jersey
Channel Islands
Tel: (0534) 68999

Channel Television
branch studio:

Television Centre
St George's Place
St Peter Port
Guernsey
Channel Islands
Tel: (0481) 23451

Grampian Television
Queen's Cross
Aberdeen
Grampian AB9 2XJ
Tel: (0224) 646464

Grampian Television
branch studios:

Albany House
Dundee
Tayside DD5 1NW
Tel: (0382) 739363

Huntley Street
Inverness
Highlands IV3 5PR
Tel: (0463) 242624

Granada Television
Granada Television Centre
Manchester
Lancashire M60 9EA
Tel: 061–832 7211

**Granada Television
branch studios:**

The Granada News Centre
Albert Dock
Liverpool
Merseyside L3 4AA
Tel: 051–709 3389

The Granada News Centre
White Cross
Lancaster
Lancashire LA1 4XQ
Tel: (0524) 60688

The Granada News Centre
Lower Bridge Street
Chester
Cheshire CH1 1SA
Tel: (0244) 313966

HTV Cymru Wales
The Television Centre
Culverhouse Cross
Cardiff
South Glamorgan CF5 7XJ
Tel: (0222) 590590

London Weekend Television
South Bank Television
 Centre
Upper Ground
London SE1 9LT
Tel: 071–620 1620

Meridian Broadcasting
Television Centre
Southampton
Hampshire SO9 5HZ
Tel: (0703) 222555

Scottish Television
Cowcaddens
Glasgow
Strathclyde G2 3PR
Tel: 041–332 9999

**Scottish Television
branch studio:**

The Gateway
Edinburgh
Midlothian EH1 4AH
Tel: 031–557 4554

Tyne Tees
The Television Centre
City Road
Newcastle upon Tyne
Tyne & Wear NE1 2AL
Tel: 091–261 0181

Ulster Television
Havelock House
Ormeau Road
Belfast
County Antrim BT7 1EB
Tel: (0232) 328122

Westcountry Television
Western Wood Way
Language Science Park
Plymouth
Devon PL7 5BG
Tel: (0752) 333333

Yorkshire Television
Television Centre
Leeds
West Yorkshire LS3 1JS
Tel: (0532) 438283

**Yorkshire Television
branch studios:**

Charter Square
Sheffield
South Yorkshire S1 3EJ
Tel: (0742) 723262

23 Brook Street
The Prospect Centre
Hull
North Humberside
HU2 8PN
Tel: (0482) 24488

88 Bailgate
Lincoln
Lincolnshire LN1 3AR
Tel: (0522) 530738

8 Bullring
Grimsby
South Humberside
DN31 1DY
Tel: (0472) 357026

1 Queen Street
Ripon
North Yorkshire HG4 1EG
Tel: (0765) 701551

8 Coppergate
York
North Yorkshire YO1 1NR
Tel: (0904) 610066

121–123 High Street
Northallerton
North Yorkshire DL6 1YT
Tel: (0609) 63430

HTV West
Television Centre
Bath Road
Bristol
Avon BS4 3HG
Tel: (0272) 778366

Oracle Teletext
Craven House
25–32 Marshall Street
London W1V 8AN
Tel: 071–434 3121

Appendix 3

BBC regional radio and television

* = local studios that have television studio facilities

Scotland

BBC Scotland *
Broadcasting House
Queen Margaret Drive
Glasgow
Strathclyde G12 8DG
Tel: 041–330 2345

BBC Scotland *
Broadcasting House
Beechgrove Terrace
Aberdeen
Grampian AB9 2ZT
Tel: (0224) 625233

BBC Scotland *
Broadcasting House
5 Queen Street
Edinburgh
Midlothian EH2 1JF
Tel: 031–243 1200

BBC Dundee *
66 Nethergate
Dundee
Tayside DD1 4ER
Tel: (0382) 202481

BBC Radio Highland
7 Culduthel Road
Inverness
Highlands IV2 4AD
Tel: (0463) 221771

Radio Nan Gaidheal
Rosebank
Church Street
Stornoway
Isle of Lewis PA87 2LS
Tel: (0851) 5000

and

Clydesdale Bank Building
Portree
Isle of Skye IV51 9EH
Tel: (0478) 2005

BBC Radio Orkney
Castle Street
Kirkwall
Orkney
Isles of Orkney KW17 1DF
Tel: (0856) 3939

BBC Radio Shetland
Brentham House
Lerwick
Shetland Islands ZE1 0LR
Tel: (0595) 4747

BBC Radio Solway
Elmbank
Lover's Walk
Dumfries
Dumfries & Galloway
DG1 1NZ
Tel: (0387) 68008

BBC Radio Tweed
Municipal Buildings
High Street
Selkirk
Borders TD7 4BU
Tel: (0750) 21884

Wales

BBC Wales *
Broadcasting House
Llantrisant Road
Llantrisant
Cardiff
South Glamorgan CF5 2YQ
Tel: (0222) 572888

BBC Radio Bangor *
Broadcasting House
Meirion Road
Bangor
Gwynedd LL57 2BY
Tel: (0248) 370880

BBC Radio Clwyd
The Old School House
Glanafron Road
Mold
Clwyd CH7 1PA
Tel: (0352) 59111

BBC Radio Gwent
Powys House
Cwmbran
Gwent NP44 1YF
Tel: (0633) 872872

BBC Radio Swansea
Broadcasting House
32 Alexandra Road
Swansea
West Glamorgan SA1 5DZ
Tel: (0792) 654986

Northern Ireland

BBC Northern Ireland *
Broadcasting House
Ormeau Avenue
Belfast
County Antrim BT2 8HQ
Tel: (0232) 338000

BBC Radio Foyle
8 Northland Road
Londonderry
County Londonderry BT48
7JD
Tel: (0504) 262244

England

BBC South and East

BBC South and East *
Elstree Centre
Clarendon Road
Borehamwood
Hertfordshire WD6 1JF
Tel: 081–953 6100

BBC East *
St Catherine's Close
All Saints Green
Norwich
Norfolk NR1 3ND
Tel: (0603) 619331

BBC Radio Bedfordshire
PO Box 476
Hastings Street
Luton
Bedfordshire LU1 5BA
Tel: (0582) 459111

BBC Radio Cambridge
Broadcasting House
104 Hills Road
Cambridge
Cambridgeshire CB2 1LD
Tel: (0223) 315970

BBC Radio Essex
PO Box 765
198 London Road
Chelmsford
Essex CM2 9AB
Tel: (0245) 262393

BBC Radio Kent
Sun Pier
Chatham
Kent ME4 4EZ
Tel: (0634) 830505

BBC Radio Norfolk *
Norfolk Tower
Surrey Street
Norwich
Norfolk NR1 3PA
Tel: (0603) 617411

BBC Radio Northampton
PO Box 1107
Abingdon Street
Northampton
Northamptonshire NN1 2BE
Tel: (0602) 239100

BBC Radio Oxford
269 Banbury Road
Summerton
Oxford
Oxfordshire OX2 7DW
Tel: (0865) 311444

BBC Radio Sussex
Marlborough Place
Brighton
Sussex BN1 1TU
Tel: (0273) 680231

BBC Radio Suffolk
Broadcasting House
St Matthews Street
Ipswich
Suffolk IP1 3EP
Tel: (0473) 250000

BBC Radio Surrey
Broadcasting House
Guildford
Surrey GU2 5AP
Tel: (0483) 306113

BBC GLR (Greater London)
35a Marylebone High Street
London W1A 4LG
Tel: 071–224 2000

BBC North

BBC North *
New Broadcasting House
PO Box 27
Oxford Road
Manchester
Lancashire M60 1SJ
Tel: 061–200 2020

BBC Radio Cleveland
PO Box 1548
Broadcasting House
Newport Road
Middlesborough
Cleveland TS1 5DG
Tel: (0642) 225211

BBC Radio Cumbria *
Hilltop Heights
London Road
Carlisle
Cumbria CA1 2NA
Tel: (0228) 31661

BBC Radio Furness
Broadcasting House
Hartington Street
Barrow in Furness
Cumbria LA14 5SH
Tel: (0229) 36767

GMR *
Oxford Road
Manchester
Lancashire M60 1SJ
Tel: 061–200 2000

BBC Radio Humberside
63 Jameson Street
Hull
North Humberside
HU1 3NU
Tel: (0482) 23232

BBC Radio Lancashire
Darwen Street
Blackburn
Lancashire BB2 2EA
Tel: (0254) 62411

BBC Radio Leeds *
Broadcasting House
Woodhouse Lane
Leeds
West Yorkshire LS2 9PN
Tel: (0532) 442131

BBC Radio Merseyside
55 Paradise Street
Liverpool
Merseyside L1 3BP
Tel: 051–708 5500

BBC Radio Newcastle *
Broadcasting Centre
Barrack Road
Newcastle upon Tyne
Tyne & Wear NE99 1RN
Tel: 091–232 4141

BBC Radio Sheffield
Ashdell Grove
60 Westbourne Road
Sheffield
South Yorkshire S10 2QU
Tel: (0742) 686185

BBC Radio York
20 Bootham Row
York
North Yorkshire YO3 7BR
Tel: (0904) 641351

BBC Midlands

BBC Midlands *
Broadcasting Centre
Pebble Mill
Birmingham
West Midlands B5 7QQ
Tel: 021–414 8888

BBC Radio Derby
56 St Helen's Street
Derby
Derbyshire DE1 3HY
Tel: (0332) 381111

**BBC Radio Hereford &
  Worcester**
Hylton Road
Worcester
Hereford & Worcester
WR2 5WW
Tel: (0905) 748485

and

43 Broad Street
Hereford
Hereford & Worcester
HR4 9HH
Tel: (0432) 56448

BBC Radio Leicester
Epic House
Charles Street
Leicester
Leicestershire LE1 3SH
Tel: (0533) 516688

BBC Radio Lincolnshire
Radion Buildings
Newport
Lincoln
Lincolnshire LN1 3XY
Tel: (0522) 511411

BBC Radio CWR
25 Warwick Road
Coventry
West Midlands CV1 2WR
Tel: (0203) 559911

BBC Radio Nottingham *
York House
Mansfield Road
Nottingham
Nottinghamshire NG1 3JB
Tel: (0602) 415161

BBC Radio Shropshire
2–4 Boscobel Drive
Shrewsbury
Shropshire SY1 3TT
Tel: (0743) 271702

BBC Radio Stoke
Conway House
Cheapside
Henley
Stoke on Trent
Stafffordshire ST1 1JJ
Tel: (0782) 208080

BBC Radio WM *
PO Box 206
Pebble Mill
Birmingham
West Midlands B5 7SD
Tel: 021–414 8484

BBC South and West

BBC South and West *
Broadcasting House
Whiteladies Road
Bristol
Avon BS8 2LR
Tel: (0272) 732211

BBC South *
South Western House
Canute Road
Southampton
Hampshire SO9 1PF
Tel: (0707) 226201

BBC South West *
Broadcasting House
Seymour Road
Mannamead
Plymouth
Devon PL3 5BD
Tel: (0752) 229201

BBC Radio Bristol
3 Tyndalls Park Road
Bristol
Avon BS8 1PP
Tel: (0272) 741111

Somerset Sound
15 Paul Street
Taunton
Somerset TA1 3PF
Tel: (0823) 252437

BBC Radio Cornwall
Phoenix Wharf
Truro
Cornwall TR1 1UA
Tel: (0872) 754210

BBC Radio Devon
PO Box 100
St David's Hill
Exeter
Devon EX4 4DB
Tel: (0392) 215651

BBC Radio Gloucestershire
London Road
Gloucester
Gloucestershire GL1 1SW
Tel: (0452) 308585

BBC Radio Solent
South Western House
Canute Road
Southampton
Hampshire SO9 4PJ
Tel: (0703) 631311

BBC Wiltshire Sound
Broadcasting House
Prospect Place
Swindon
Wiltshire SN1 3RW
Tel: (0793) 513626

BBC Radio Guernsey
Commerce House
Les Banques
St Peter Port
Guernsey
Channel Islands
Tel: (0481) 28977

BBC Radio Jersey
Broadcasting House
Rouge Bouillon
St Helier
Jersey
Channel Islands
Tel: (0534) 70000

Appendix 4

Independent local radio

Greater London

Capital FM
Euston Tower
Euston Road
London NW1 3DR
Tel: 071–388 1288

Capital Gold
Euston Tower
Euston Road
London NW1 3DR
Tel: 071–388 1288

Choice FM
16–18 Trinity Gardens
London SW9
Tel: 071–738 7969

London Greek Radio
Florentina Village
Vale Road
London N4 1TD
Tel: 081–800 8001

Jazz FM
The Jazz House
Castlereagh Street
London W1H 5YR
Tel: 071–706 4100

Kiss FM
Kiss House
80 Holloway Road
London N7 8JG
Tel: 071–700 6100

LBC Newstalk
Crown House
72 Hammersmith Road
London W14 8YE
Tel: 071–603 2400

LBC Talkback
Crown House
72 Hammersmith Road
London W14 8YE
Tel: 071–371 1515

Melody Radio
1 Grosvenor Place
London SW1X 7JN
Tel: 071–823 1018

RTM 103
17–20 Tavy Bridge
London SE2 9UG
Tel: 081–311 3112

Spectrum Radio
Endeavour House
Brent Cross
London NW2 1JT
Tel: 081–905 5000

Sunrise Radio
PO Box 212
Hounslow
Middlesex TW3 2AD

WNK Radio
185b High Road
Wood Green
London N22 6BA
Tel: 081–889 1547

Midlands

Beacon Radio
267 Tettenhall Road
Wolverhampton
West Midlands WV6 0DQ
Tel: (0902) 757211

BRMB
PO Box 555
Aston North Road
Birmingham
West Midlands B6 4BX
Tel: 021–359 4481

Buzz FM
20 Augusta Street
Jewellery Quarter
Birmingham
West Midlands B18 6JA
Tel: 021–236 0258

Echo 96
Studio 257
Stoke Road
Stoke-on-Trent
Staffordshire ST4 2SR
Tel: (0782) 747047

Gem AM
29–31 Castle Gate
Nottingham
Nottinghamshire NG1 7AP
Tel: (0602) 588614

Marcher Sound Classic Hits
The Studios
Mold Road
Wrexham
Clwyd LL11 4AF
Tel: (0978) 752202

Mercia-FM
Hertford Place
Coventry
West Midlands CV1 3TT
Tel: (0203) 633933

MFM 1034
5 Upper Northgate
Chester
Cheshire CH1 4EE
Tel: (0244) 390101

Nice 'n' Easy WABC
PO Box 303
267 Tettenhall Road
Wolverhampton
West Midlands WV6 0DQ
Tel: (0902) 757211

Northants Radio
71 Abingdon Street
Northampton
Northamptonshire
NN1 2HW
Tel: (0604) 29811

Radio Harmony
Ringway House
Hill Street
Coventry
West Midlands CV1 4AN
Tel: (0203) 525656

Radio Wyvern
5 Barbourne Terrace
Worcester
Hereford and Worcester
WR1 3JZ
Tel: (0905) 612212

Signal Radio
Studio 257
Stoke Road
Stoke-on-Trent
Staffordshire ST4 2SR
Tel: (0782) 747047

Sound FM
Granville House
Granville Road
Leicester
Leicestershire LE1 7RW
Tel: (0533) 551616

Trent FM (Derby)
The Market Place
Derby
Derbyshire DE1 3AA
Tel: (0332) 292945

Trent FM (Nottingham)
29–31 Castle Gate
Nottingham
Nottinghamshire NG1 7AP
Tel: (0602) 581731

Xtra-AM
PO Box 555
Aston Road North
Birmingham
West Midlands B6 4BX
Tel: 021–359 4481

North East

Aire FM
PO Box 2000
51 Burley Road
Leeds
West Yorkshire LS3 1LR
Tel: (0532) 452299

Classic Gold
South Yorkshire Studio
PO Box 194
Hartshead
Sheffield
South Yorkshire S1 1GP
Tel: (0742) 721021

and

West Yorkshire Studio
PO Box 235
Pennine House
Forster Square
Bradford
West Yorkshire BD1 5NP
Tel: (0274) 394045

Great North Radio
Humberside and East
  Yorkshire Studio
Commercial Road
Hull
North Humberside
HU1 1SG
Tel: (0482) 219199

Metro FM
Swalwell
Newcastle upon Tyne
Tyen & Wear NE99 1BB
Tel: 091–488 3131

Metro FM
branch studio:

74 Dovecott Street
Stockton-on-Tees
Cleveland TS18 1HB
Tel: (0642) 615111

Radio Borders
Tweedside Park
Galashiels
Selkirk
Borders TD1 3TD
Tel: (0896) 59444

TFM Radio
74 Dovecott Street
Stockton-on-Tees
Cleveland TS18 1HB
Tel: (0642) 615111

Viking FM
Commercial Road
Hull
North Humberside
HU1 2SG
Tel: (0482) 25141

Wear FM
Forster Building
Sunderland Polytechnic
Chester Street
Sunderland
Tyne & Wear SR1 3SD
Tel: 091–515 2103

North West

BCR FM
30 Chapel Street
Little Germany
Bradford
West Yorkshire BD1 5DN
Tel: (0274) 735043

City-FM
PO Box 467
Liverpool
Merseyside L69 1TQ
Tel: 051–227 5100

City-Talk
PO Box 467
Liverpool
Merseyside L69 1TQ
Tel: 051–227 5100

Hallam FM
PO Box 194
Hartshead
Sheffield
South Yorkshire S1 1GP

Key 103
127-131 The Piazza
Piccadilly Plaza
Manchester
Lancashire M1 4AW
Tel: 061–236 9913

KFM Radio
Regent House
Heaton Lane
Stockport
Cheshire SK4 1BX
Tel: 061–480 5445

Magic 828
PO Box 2000
51 Burley Road
Leeds
West Yorkshire LS3 1LR
Tel: (0532) 452299

Manx Radio
Broadcasting House
Douglas
Isle of Man
Tel: (0624) 661411

Pennine Radio
PO Box 235
Pennine House
Forster Square
Bradford
West Yorkshire BD1 5NP
Tel: (0274) 731521

Piccadilly Radio
127–131 The Piazza
Piccadilly Plaza
Manchester
Lancashire M1 4AW
Tel: 061–236 9913

Red Rose Gold
St Paul's Square
Preston
Lancashire PR1 1YE
Tel: (0772) 556301

Red Rose Rock FM
St Paul's Square
Preston
Lancashire PR1 1YE
Tel: (0772) 556301

Sunset Radio
23 New Mount Street
Manchester
Lancashire M4 4DE
Tel: 061–953 5353

South East

Breeze AM
PO Box 300
Southend-on-Sea
Essex SS1 1SY
Tel: (0702) 430966

CRMK
The Old Rectory
Waterside
Peartree Bridge
Milton Keynes
Buckinghamshire MK6 3EJ
Tel: (0908) 667419

CNFM 103
PO Box 1000
Vision Park
Histon
Cambridge
Cambridgeshire CB4 4WW
Tel: (0223) 235255

Chiltern Radio
Chiltern Road
Dunstable
Bedfordshire LU1 1HQ
Tel: (0582) 661725

**Chiltern Radio
branch studio:**

Goldington Road
Bedford
Bedfordshire MK40 3LS
Tel: (0234) 272400

Coast Classics
37 Earl Street
Maidstone
Kent ME14 1PF
Tel: (0622) 679061

Delta Radio
Chertsey Road
Woking
Surrey GU21 5XY
Tel: (0483) 740066

First Gold Radio
Chertsey Road
Woking
Surrey GU21 5XY
Tel: (0483) 740066

Premier Radio
Chertsey Road
Woking
Surrey GU21 5XY
Tel: (0483) 740066

Essex Radio
Radio House
19–20 Clifftown Road
Southend-on-Sea
Essex SS1 1SX
Tel: (0702) 333711

**Essex Radio
branch studio:**

Radio House
53 Duke Street
Chelmsford
Essex CM1 1SX
Tel: (0245) 251141

First Gold Radio
Chertsey Road
Woking
Surrey GU21 5XY
Tel: (0483) 740753

Fox FM
Bush House
Pony Road
Cowley
Oxford
Oxfordshire OX4 2XR
Tel: (0865) 748721

Hereward Radio
PO Box 225
Queensgate Centre
Peterborough
Cambridgeshire PE1 1KJ
Tel: (0733) 46225

Horizon
Broadcasting Centre
Crownhill
Milton Keynes
Buckinghamshire MK8 0AB
Tel: (0908) 269111

Invicta Radio
15 Station Road East
Canterbury
Kent CT1 2RB
Tel: (0227) 767661

**Invicta Radio
branch studio:**

37 Earl Street
Maidstone
Kent ME14 1PF
Tel: (0622) 679061

Mellow 1557
21–23 Walton Road
Frinton-on-Sea
Essex CO13 0AA
Tel: (0225) 675303

Northants Radio
71 Abingdon Street
Northampton
Northamptonshire
NN1 2HW
Tel: (0604) 29811

Orwell Radio
Electric House
Lloyds Avenue
Ipswich
Suffolk IP1 3HZ
Tel: (0473) 216971

Radio Broadland
St George's Plain
Colegate
Norwich
Norfolk NR3 1DB
Tel: (0603) 630621

**Radio Broadland
branch studio:**

5 Stonecutters Way
Great Yarmouth
Norfolk NR29 1HF
Tel: (0493) 854875

Radio Mercury
Broadfield House
Brighton Road
Crawley
West Sussex RH11 9TT
Tel: (0993) 519161

Saxon FM
Long Brackland
Bury St Edmunds
Suffolk IP33 1JY
Tel: (0284) 701511

Southern Sound FM
PO Box 2000
Brighton
East Sussex BN41 2SS
Tel: (0273) 430111

210 FM
PO Box 210
Reading
Berkshire RG3 5RZ
Tel: (0734) 413131

South and West

Brunel Radio
PO Box 2020
Bristol
Avon BS99 7SN
Tel: (0272) 279900

DevonAir
Studio Centre
33–37 St David's Hill
Exeter
Devon EX4 4DA
Tel: (0392) 430703

FTP
25 Portland Square
Bristol
Avon BS2 8RZ
Tel: (0272) 240111

Gold FM
Whittle Avenue
Segensworth West
Fareham
Hampshire PO15 5PA
Tel: (0489) 589911

GWR FM
PO Box 2000
Swindon
Wiltshire SN4 7EX
Tel: (0793) 853222

Isle of Wight Radio
Dodnor Park
Newport
Isle of Wight
Tel: (0983) 822557

Light FM
Whittle Avenue
Segensworth West
Fareham
Hampshire PO15 5PA
Tel: (0489) 589911

Ocean Sound
Segensworth West
Whittle Avenue
Fareham
Hampshire PO15 5PA
Tel: (0489) 589911

Orchard FM
Taunton
Somerset TA3 7BT
Tel: (0823) 338448

Plymouth Sound
Earl's Acre
Plymouth
Devon PL3 4HX
Tel: (0752) 227272

Power FM
Whittle Avenue
Segensworth West
Fareham
Hampshire PO15 5PA
Tel: (0489) 589911

Severn Sound FM
PO Box 388
Gloucester
Gloucestershire GL1 2DQ
Tel: (0452) 423791

South West 103
Studio Centre
35–37 St David's Hill
Exeter
Devon EX4 4DA
Tel: (0392) 430703

Three Counties Radio
PO Box 388
Gloucester
Gloucestershire GL1 2DQ
Tel: (0452) 423791

Two Counties Radio
Southcote Road
Bournemouth
Dorset BH1 3LR
Tel: (0202) 294881

210 FM
PO Box 210
Reading
Berkshire RG3 5RZ
Tel: (0734) 413131

Scotland

Centresound
Stirling Enterprise Park
John Player Building
Kerse Road
Stirling
Central FK6 7RP
Tel: (0786) 51188

Clyde FM
Clydebank Business Park
Glasgow
Strathclyde G81 2RX
Tel: 041–941 1111

East End Radio
GEBC
19 Blairtommock Road
Glasgow
Strathclyde G33 4AN
Tel: 041–774 5335

Max AM
Forth House
Forth Street
Edinburgh
Lothian EH1 3LF
Tel: 031–558 3277

Moray Firth Radio
PO Box 271
Inverness
Highlands IV3 6SF
Tel: (0463) 224433

North Sound Radio
45 King's Gate
Aberdeen
Grampian AB2 6BL
Tel: (0224) 632234

Radio Borders
Tweedside Park
Galashiels
Selkirk
Borders TD1 3TD
Tel: (0896) 59444

Radio Borders
branch studio:

Berwick Studio
The Maltings Art Centre
Berwick-upon-Tweed
Northumberland
Tel: (0289) 307464

Radio Clyde
Clydebank Business Park
Glasgow
Strathclyde G81 2RX
Tel: 041–306 2200

Radio Forth
Forth House
Forth Street
Edinburgh
Lothian EH1 3LF
Tel: 031–556 9255

Radio Tay
PO Box 123
Dundee
Tayside DD1 9UF
Tel: (0382) 200800

South West Radio
Campbell House
Bankend Road
Dumfries
Dumfries and Galloway
DG1 4TH
Tel: (0387) 65629

West Sound
Campbell House
Bankend Road
Dumfries
Dumfries and Galloway
DG1 4TH
Tel: (0387) 58999

West Sound Radio
Radio House
Holmston Road
Ayr
Strathclyde KA7 3BE
Tel: (0292) 283662

Wales

Marcher Sound
The Studios
Mold Road
Wrexham
Clwyd LL11 4AF
Tel: (0978) 752202

Radio Wyvern
5–6 Barbourne Terrace
Worcester
Hereford and Worcester
WR1 3JS
Tel: (0905) 612212

Red Dragon Radio
PO Box 221
West Canal Wharf
Cardiff
South Glamorgan CF1 5XJ
Tel: (0222) 384041

Touch AM
PO Box 99
West Canal Wharf
Cardiff
South Glamorgan CF1 5XJ
Tel: (0222) 384014

Swansea Sound
Victoria Road
Gowerton
Swansea
West Glamorgan SA4 3AB
Tel: (0792) 893751

Northern Ireland

BCR
Russell Court Complex
Claremont Street
Belfast
Country Antrim BT9 6JX
Tel: (0232) 438500

Cool FM
PO Box 974
Belfast
County Antrim BT1 1RT
Tel: (0247) 817171

Downtown Radio
Newtownards
County Down BT23 4ES
Tel: (0247) 815555

Index